7th Workshop on NLP for Computer Assisted Language Learning (NLP4CALL 2018)

NEALT Proceedings Series Volume 36

Stockholm, Sweden
7 November 2018

Editors:

Ildiko Pilan
David Alfter

Elena Volodina
Lars Borin

ISBN: 978-1-5108-7752-8

Proceedings of the

7th Workshop on NLP for Computer Assisted Language Learning (NLP4CALL 2018)

at SLTC 2018
Stockholm, 7th November 2018

edited by

Ildikó Pilán, Elena Volodina, David Alfter and Lars Borin

Linköping Electronic Conference Proceedings   152
eISSN 1650-3740 (Online) • ISSN 1650-3686 (Print)   2018

Preface

The primary goal of the workshop series on Natural Language Processing for Computer-Assisted Language Learning (NLP4CALL) is to create a meeting place for researchers working on the integration of Natural Language Processing and Speech Technologies in CALL systems and exploring the theoretical and methodological issues arising in this connection. The latter includes, among others, insights from Second Language Acquisition (SLA) research, on the one hand, and promoting the development of "Computational SLA" through setting up Second Language research infrastructure(s), on the other.

The intersection of Natural Language Processing (or Language Technology / Computational Linguistics) and Speech Technology with Computer-Assisted Language Learning (CALL) brings "understanding" of language to CALL tools, thus making CALL intelligent. This fact has given the name for this area of research – Intelligent CALL, ICALL. As the definition suggests, apart from having excellent knowledge of Natural Language Processing and/or Speech Technology, ICALL researchers need good insights into second language acquisition theories and practices, as well as knowledge of second language pedagogy and didactics. This workshop invites therefore a wide range of ICALL-relevant research, including studies where NLP-enriched tools are used for testing SLA and pedagogical theories, and vice versa, where SLA theories, pedagogical practices or empirical data are modeled in ICALL tools. The NLP4CALL workshop series is aimed at bringing together competencies from these areas for sharing experiences and brainstorming around the future of the field.

We invited submissions:

- that describe research directly aimed at ICALL;
- that demonstrate actual or discuss the potential use of existing Language and Speech Technologies or resources for language learning;
- that describe the ongoing development of resources and tools with potential usage in ICALL, either directly in interactive applications, or indirectly in materials, application or curriculum development, e.g. learning material generation, assessment of learner texts/responses, individualized learning solutions, provision of feedback;
- that discuss challenges and/or research agenda for ICALL;
- that describe empirical studies on language learner data.

A special focus was given to established and upcoming infrastructures aimed at SLA and learner corpus research, covering questions such as data collection, legal issues, reliability of annotation, annotation tool development and search environments for SLA-relevant data. We encouraged paper presentations and software demonstrations describing the above-mentioned themes primarily, but not exclusively, for the Nordic languages.

This year, we had the pleasure to welcome two invited speakers: Jill Burstein (Educational Testing Service) and Jan Hulstijn (University of Amsterdam).

Jill Burstein is a Research Director of the Natural Language Processing Group in Research & Development at Educational Testing Service in Princeton, New Jersey. Her research interests span Natural Language Processing for educational technology, automated essay scoring and evaluation, discourse and sentiment analysis, argumentation mining, education policy, English language learning, and writing research. The intersection of her interests has led to two extensively used commercial applications for English L2 learners: E-rater®, ETS' automated essay evaluation application, and the Language Muse Activity Palette™ - a new classroom tool under development targeting English learners that automatically generates

Ildikó Pilán, Elena Volodina, David Alfter and Lars Borin 2018. Preface. *Proceedings of the 7th Workshop on NLP for Computer Assisted Language Learning at SLTC 2018 (NLP4CALL 2018)*. Linköping Electronic Conference Proceedings 152: i–v.

language activities for classroom texts to support content comprehension. Jill Burstein is one of the most successful researchers within ICALL that together with a group of bright researchers made ICALL tools a reality for many teachers of L2 English.

In her talk, *Natural Language Processing for Education: Applications for Reading and Writing Proficiency*, she explored automated writing evaluation (or, AWE) systems, which have been largely used to support the measurement of writing skills for on-demand, large-volume, high-stakes assessments. She argued that advances in natural language processing (NLP)-driven AWE now affords the ability, in real-time, to generate a variety of linguistic information which can provide support literacy for reading and writing. NLP-based technology can now be used to 1) build a broader array of capabilities to support the instruction for a diverse population of learners, and 2) offer educational analytics for various stakeholders, including students, instructors, parents, administrators and policy-makers. Her talk discussed the history of AWE, the literacy-based motivation and trajectory for AWE-driven technology development, two technology use cases of AWE-based reading (The Language Muse® Activity Palette) and writing applications (The Writing Mentor™), and exploratory research examining relationships between linguistic features in college writing and broader success predictors that can potentially inform continued development of technology that supports literacy.

Jan Hulstijn is professor emeritus of second language acquisition at the Amsterdam Center for Language and Communication (ACLC) of the University of Amsterdam. He has been affiliated with this university (full professor) since 1998. Before that he held positions at Leiden University and the Free University of Amsterdam. He was associate post-doc researcher at the University of Toronto, Canada (1982-1983) and he was visiting professor at the University of Leuven, Belgium, (2002) and at Stockholm University (2005). His main research interests are concerned with (1) language proficiency in native and non-native speakers; (2) explicit versus implicit accounts of first and second language learning and (3) theories of second language acquisition and philosophy of science. With others PIs, he received a number of research grants from the Netherlands Organisation of Scientific Research (NWO) between 1982 and 2007 (see webpage). In 2018 he received the 2018 distinguished scholar award from the European Second Language Association (EuroSLA) (http://www.eurosla.org/distinguished-scholar-award-2018-jan-h-hulstijn/). In 2015, he published a book presenting his theory of basic language cognition (BLC).

His talk was entitled *Usage-based views on second language acquisition and the Common European Framework of Reference (CEFR): their potential relevance for the NLP field.* The first wave of the Cognitive Revolution (1960 – 1985) was dominated by (1) the competence-performance distinction and Universal Grammar in generative linguistics, and by (2) notions of modularity and serial processing in psycholinguistics. These notions also dominated the scientific study of second language acquisition (SLA) at the time. In contrast, more recent work in SLA is increasingly being influenced by ideas which originated during the second wave of the Cognitive Revolution (1985 – the present), in particular usage-based linguistics, Emergentism and the Competition Model, Construction Grammar, Dynamic Systems Theory, implicit/statistical learning, and statistical learning in relation to corpus linguistics. These developments might be important for people working in the field of NLP. In the first part of his talk he gave a brief overview of these more recent developments, with a particular focus on the unified conceptualization of representation and processing (referred to together with the term cognition), the notion of graded cognition (as opposed to dichotomous views of cognition), the notion of frequency and recency of linguistic elements in learners' input (with the aid of corpus linguistics), the removal of traditional barriers between lexis and grammar, and the need to explain individual differences in language knowledge and use. In his view, current software for automatic analysis of corpora of spoken or written language production is still incapable of identifying grammatical constructions relevant from an SLA perspective. The notions of shared/basic and non-shared/extended language cognition were also briefly introduced (Hulstijn, 2015, 2018). In the final part of his talk, he presented his views on the Common European Framework of Reference for Language (CEFR, 2001), which currently dominates almost all practices in second-language testing in Europe and whose presence has been increasing also in other parts of the world.

> Hulstijn, J. H. (2015). *Language proficiency in native and non-native speakers: Theory and research*. Amsterdam: John Benjamins Publishing Company.
>
> Hulstijn, J.H. (2018, early view). An individual-differences framework for comparing non-native with native speakers: Perspectives from BLC Theory. *Language Learning*. DOI: 10.1111/lang.12317

Previous workshops

This workshop follows a series of workshops on NLP for CALL organized by the NEALT Special Interest Group on Intelligent Computer-Assisted Language Learning (SIG-ICALL[1]). The workshop series has previously been financed by the Center for Language Technology[2] at the University of Gothenburg, and the Swedish Research Council's conference grant.

Submissions to the seven workshop editions have targeted a wide variety of languages, ranging from well-resourced languages (Chinese, German, English, French, Portuguese, Russian, Spanish) to less-resourced ones (Erzya, Arabic, Estonian, Irish, Komi-Zyrian, Meadow Mari, Saami, Udmurt, Võro). Among these several Nordic languages have been targeted: Danish, Estonian, Finnish, Icelandic, Norwegian, Saami, Swedish, and Võro. The wide scope is also evident in the affiliations of the participating authors as shown in Table 1:

---

[1] https://spraakbanken.gu.se/swe/forskning/ICALL/SIG-ICALL
[2] http://clt.gu.se/

Country	# authors
Australia	2
Belgium	4
Canada	3
Denmark	1
Estonia	3
Finland	7
France	3
Germany	57
Iceland	3
Ireland	2
Japan	2
Norway	12
Portugal	4
Russia	10
Slovakia	1
Spain	3
Sweden	62
Switzerland	10
UK	1
US	3

Table 1: Authors by affiliation country, 2012-2018

During the past years, the acceptance rate has varied between 50% and 77%, the average being 65% (see Table 2). The acceptance rate is rather high, however, the reviewing process has always been very rigorous, with two or three double-blind reviews per submission. This indicates that submissions to the workshops have usually been of high quality.

Workshop year	Submitted	Accepted	Acceptance rate
2012	12	8	67%
2013	8	4	50%
2014	13	10	77%
2015	9	6	67%
2016	14	10	72%
2017	13	7	54%
2018	16	11	69%

Table 2: Submission and acceptance rates, 2012-2018

We would like to thank our Program Committee for providing detailed feedback for the reviewed papers:

- Lars Ahrenberg, Linköping University, Sweden
- David Alfter, University of Gothenburg, Sweden
- Lisa Beinborn, University of Duisburg-Essen, Germany
- Eckhard Bick, University of Southern Denmark, Denmark
- António Branco, University of Lisbon, Portugal

- Jill Burstein, Educational Testing Services, US
- Andrew Caines, University of Cambridge, UK
- Dirk De Hertog, KU Leuven, Belgium
- Simon Dobnik, University of Gothenburg, Sweden
- Thomas François, UCLouvain, Belgium
- Johannes Graën, University of Zurich, Switzerland
- Andrea Horbach, University of Duisburg-Essen, Germany
- John Lee, City University of Hong Kong, Hong Kong
- Peter Ljunglöf, University of Gothenburg and Chalmers University of Technology, Sweden
- Montse Maritxalar, University of the Basque country, Spain
- Beáta Megyesi, Uppsala University, Sweden
- Detmar Meurers, University of Tübingen, Germany
- Martí Quixal, University of Tübingen, Germany
- Robert Reynolds, Brigham Young University, USA
- Gerold Schneider, University of Zurich, Switzerland
- Irina Temnikova, Sofia University, Bulgaria
- Francis Tyers, The Arctic University of Norway, Norway
- Sowmya Vajjala, Iowa State University, US
- Elena Volodina, University of Gothenburg, Sweden
- Mats Wirén, Stockholm University, Sweden
- Victoria Yaneva, University of Wolverhampton, UK
- Torsten Zesch, University of Duisburg-Essen, Germany
- Robert Östling, University of Helsinki, Finland

We intend to continue this workshop series, which so far has been the only ICALL-relevant recurring event based in the Nordic countries. Our intention is to co-locate the workshop series with the two major LT events in Scandinavia, SLTC (the Swedish Language Technology Conference) and NoDaLiDa (Nordic Conference on Computational Linguistics), thus making this workshop an annual event. Through this workshop, we intend to profile ICALL research in Nordic countries as well as beyond, and we aim at providing a dissemination venue for researchers active in this area.

Workshop website:
https://spraakbanken.gu.se/eng/icall/7th-nlp4call

Workshop organizers
Ildikó Pilán, Elena Volodina, David Alfter, Lars Borin
Språkbanken, University of Gothenburg

Acknowledgements

We gratefully acknowledge the financial support from *SweLL infrastructure project on Swedish Second language*[3] regarding the invited speaker Jill Burstein, and the project on *Development of lexical and grammatical competences in immigrant Swedish*[4], that provided funding for our other invited speaker, Jan Hulstijn.

---

[3] https://spraakbanken.gu.se/eng/swell_infra, https://rj.se/anslag/2016/swell---forskningsinfrastruktur-for-svenska-som-andrasprak/

[4] https://rj.se/en/anslag/2017/utveckling-av-lexikala-och-grammatiska-kompetenser-i-invandrarsvenska/, https://spraakbanken.gu.se/eng/l2-profiling

Contents

Using authentic texts for grammar exercises for a minority language

Lene Antonsen
UiT The Arctic
University of Norway
lene.antonsen@uit.no

Chiara Argese
UiT The Arctic
University of Norway
chiara.argese@uit.no

Abstract

This paper presents an ATICALL (Authentic Text ICALL) system with automatic visual input enhancement activities for training complex inflection systems in a minority language. We have adapted the freely available VIEW system which was designed to automatically generate activities from any web content.

Our system is based on finite state transducers (FST) and Constraint Grammar, originally built for other purposes. The paper describes ways of handling ambiguity in the target form in the exercises, and ways of handling the challenges for VIEW posed by authentic text, typical for a minority language: variations in orthography, and large proportion of non-normative forms.

1 Introduction

This paper presents an implementation of an ATICALL (Authentic Text ICALL) system with automatic visual input enhancement activities for students acquiring complex inflection systems. The system, called VIEW, was originally designed to automatically generate activities from any web content for English, Spanish and German (Meurers et al., 2011), and an adaption of the browser-extension version of the program for Russian was presented by Reynolds et al. (2014). We have adapted and implemented the web-version of the program for North Saami.

Adapting the ATICALL-program to a morphology-rich minority language with a short tradition of literacy, like North Saami, gave us challenges like finding suitable texts on the internet, and finding ways of handling

both variation in orthography and large proportions of non-normative forms in the texts, in addition to making solutions for using also ambiguous grammatical forms as target words for the exercises.

The paper is structured as follows: Section 2 presents the background and motivation for our approach and puts it in a wider context. Section 3 presents the system and how it was adapted to North Saami. Section 4 discusses how we adapted the system to handle challenges related to the situation for this minority language. Section 5 contains a user evaluation, and in section 6 we present the conclusion. Finally, in section 7, we present some future perspectives.

2 Background

2.1 North Saami

North Saami is a morphology-rich language, with nominal inflection for two numbers, six cases, and possession. Nouns have paradigms both with possessive declension and without possession indicated (absolute declension), see table 1. Verbs have 45 finite forms including three persons for singular, dual and plural, in four modi (indicative, imperative, conditional, potential), and two tenses for indicative. The verbs are also inflected for ten different non-finite forms. Nouns, adjectives and verbs may be divided into groups according to stem type, each type having different paradigms. Suffixation is accompanied by phonological alternations, one of these alternations is a stem consonant alternating process, consonant gradation, where each stem may appear in two or even three versions, e.g. *gieht-, gied-, giht-* ("hand-"), as in table 1. Usually, the case suffix is sufficient to identify the case form, but for some common forms, consonant gradation is the only distinguishing feature be-

Lene Antonsen and Chiara Argese 2018. Using authentic texts for grammar exercises for a minority language. *Proceedings of the 7th Workshop on NLP for Computer Assisted Language Learning at SLTC 2018 (NLP4CALL 2018).* Linköping Electronic Conference Proceedings 152: 1–9.

tween the forms, like for *giehta, gieđa* in table 1. See Sammallahti (1998) for more information about the language.

Number and case	Even stem	Odd stem	Contracted stem
Singular:			
Nominative	*giehta*	*beana*	*suolu*
Accusative	*gieđa*	*beatnaga*	*sullo*
Illative	*gihtii*	*beatnagii*	*sullui*
Locative	*gieđas*	*beatnagis*	*sullos*
Comitative	*gieđain*	*beatnagiin*	*sulluin*
Plural:			
Nominative	*gieđat*	*beatnagat*	*sullot*
Accusative	*gieđaid*	*beatnagiid*	*sulluid*
Illative	*gieđaide*	*beatnagiidda*	*sulluide*
Locative	*gieđain*	*beatnagiin*	*sulluin*
Comitative	*gieđaiguin*	*beatnagiiguin*	*sulluiguin*
Essive	*giehtan*	*beanan*	*suolun*
In English	"hand"	"dog"	"island"

Table 1: Absolute declension of nouns in North Saami, for the three different stem types. The accusative and genitive cases are syncretic.

North Saami has approx. 20 000 speakers living in three countries, Norway, Sweden and Finland, and got a common orthography in 1978. The language is taught as native and foreign language in school and universities.

2.2 ICALL for North Saami

There are other ICALL systems for North Saami, which generate question-answer pairs with fill-in-the-blank (Antonsen et al., 2013) and question-answer drills with to some extent free input (Antonsen, 2013b). They use finite-state transducers, which make it possible to generate a virtually unlimited set of exercises, and they cover all types of combinations of stem types and inflection forms, also those which are infrequent in the texts electronically available.

Despite the availability of the question-answering systems, we still think that also an ICALL program based on authentic texts would be useful for the learners. The advantages of this new system are interesting topics for learners, more context for the exercises, and more variation in sentences with focus on frequent forms and idioms.

2.3 Based on VIEW

The system architecture is based on the VIEW (Visual Input Enhancement of the Web)[1] system described in (Meurers et al., 2011). VIEW is an ATICALL system designed to help learners in their language learning process, and it automatically produces exercises based on a text chosen by the user on the web.

Figure 1: The topic is nouns: all the target words are highlighted.

VIEW includes four different types of activities. Two activities are based on the assumption that noticing is necessary in language learning for adults (Schmidt, 1990). The learner is fist exposed for the grammatical forms: the `highlight`-activity adds colour to target wordforms, as in figure 1. The next step is when the learner looks for the forms: the `click`-activity allows the learner to find the target wordforms in the text and colorize them by clicking them.

Figure 2: The topic is nouns. The activity is to select the correct form of the target words.

The `multiple-choice`-activity allows the learner to select the correct form from a multiple-choice list, as in figure 2, and in the `practice`-activity the learner types in the wordforms. The latter will be referred to as the `cloze`-activity in this paper. The learner gets instant feedback on whether the answer is correct or not. The activities can be accessed as a web application.

2

Figure 3: Application home page, where the user can select a grammar topic from the list under Fáttát ("Topics") and an activity from the list under Hárjehusat ("Excercises"). Both of these are explained in section 2.3. From the list under Materiálat ("Materials") the learner can also choose to work with recommended web-texts, a function explained in section 4.2. Below the list there is an expand/collapse menu for adding a URL or uploading a text.

3 Implementation for North Saami

In Konteaksta[2], our implementation for North Saami (home page in figure 3), the user can choose to train her skills on four different grammatical topics:

1. Nouns
2. Finite verbforms
3. Non-finite verbforms
4. Negation form of verbs

These topics are made for the four standard VIEW activities, see 2.3. The user is then presented with three different options:

1. Choose from a set of recommended texts
2. Insert a URL of her own choice, or find one by using the "Google search" field.
3. Upload a file (explained in section 4.2).

3.1 Linguistic framework

The NLP resources being used are developed at UiT The Arctic University of Norway. They include morphological analysers implemented as finite-state transducers (FST) and compiled with the Xerox compilers TWOLC and LEXC (Beesley and Karttunen, 2003).

The syntactic parser for disambiguation and adding function tags is built within the Constraint Grammar-framework (CG) (Karlsson et al., 1995). The CG-framework is based upon manually written rule sets and a syntactic analyser which also selects the correct analysis in case of homonymy. Vislcg3 (VISL-group, 2008), a new improved version of the initial CG compiler (Karlsson, 1990; Karlsson et al., 1995), is used for compilation of the rule sets.

The North Saami analyser recognises 98% of the words in Saami texts (Antonsen and Trosterud, 2017), and has an F-score of 0.99 for part-of-speech (PoS) disambiguation, 0.94 for disambiguation of inflection and derivation, and 0.93 for assignment of grammatical functions (Antonsen et al., 2010).

3.2 Technical implementation

Our application front page is written in HTML and Javascript. Once all options have been

---

[1] The open-source research prototype is available at http://purl.org/icall/view

[2] http://oahpa.no/konteaksta/

chosen (topic, activity and webpage) the Java servlet will execute the following three steps:

1. Preprocessing. During this step the textual content from the webpage is extracted and tokenised. Then sentence boundaries are detected.

2. The text is annotated with the grammatical analyser.

3. Postprocessing. Here the target words are selected, and the HTML code is enhanced with additional attributes.

4. Loading. The enhanced page is loaded to the browser. The four different exercise types are implemented in Javascript.

One main technical issue we are facing in developing the application lies in the tokenization for sentences ending with abbreviations, as for measures, cf. "cm." in example (1). These sentences get an extra dot not present in the original text as sentence delimiter for the syntactic analysis, and this sometimes creates problems when putting each token back in its original position after it has been analysed:

(1) Darfi   berrešii leat assái, 15-25 cm.
     The turf should be   thick, 15-25 cm.
     Darfi   deaddá ...
     The turf pushes ...

As a consequence, in the text after these abbreviations, the wrong tokens are highlighted. This happens for all activities. In figure 4 nouns should be highlighted, but after the token "cm", the tokens "." and verb "deaddá" are highlighted instead of the noun "Darfi".

Darfi berrešii leat assái, 15-25 cm. Darfi deaddá

Figure 4: The output from the application when highlight-activity for nouns is chosen with text containing an abbreviation in the end of the sentence. Translation is in example (1).

This is something we are currently working with.

To take into account variation in orthography, we allowed the application to accept more forms in the cloze-activity, see 4.4 for a more detailed explanation.

To help the user focus on the text itself, we have removed the enhancement of targets in menus in the webpages (by searching and removing the enhancement from specific HTML-tags).

After initial testing, we realised that one limit of the application is its performance in terms of response time (especially for the multiple-choice and cloze activities). This was improved by the following: before the preprocess is executed the application checks whether a file with annotated text exists; if it does, only the postprocessing and loading steps are executed; if not, the output from the preprocessing is saved to a file for future use. In this way, the process is now twice as fast as before.

4   Challenges for a morphology-rich minority language

In the VIEW-versions for English and German the key-answer is the form used in the original text, which the activity is based on (Meurers et al., 2011, 13), and this is also the situation for Russian, except from the generating of words with stress marking, which is not a part of Russian orthography (Reynolds et al., 2014, 102).

For a morphology-rich language with much variation like North Saami, we chose to generate the key-answer, based on the morphological analysis of the target word, and in many cases the system will accept several answers. This is important both for target selection (section 4.1), and for variation and misspellings (section 4.4).

For a minority language there are also challenges in finding suitable web-texts (section 4.2), and there is often a mix of both the minority and the majority language in the web page (section 4.3).

4.1   Target selection

Each noun declension paradigm has 11 cells, see table 1. In the multiple-choice and cloze-activities it is not always obvious for the learner which form to choose. If there is no agreement with another member of the sentence, e.g. subject-verbal agreement, the learner will not know whether the target should be in singular or plural if there is no picture as reference. The Russian VIEW does not select tokens for which number is grammatically ambiguous (Reynolds et al., 2014, 102).

Proceedings of the 7th Workshop on NLP for Computer Assisted Language Learning at SLTC 2018 (NLP4CALL 2018)

In our first version of the program we solved the problem by dividing singular and plural nouns into two target types, so the learner would choose to work with either nouns in singular or nouns in plural. But two of the cells in the case paradigm always have homonymous forms across numbers: singular comitative and plural locative, e.g. *giedain* (Sg.Com: "with the hand" or Pl.Loc: "in the hands"). The analyser does not always succeed in choosing correctly between these two analyses, so there is a risk of using a plural target when the learner has chosen a singular activity, or the other way round. The learner is never exposed to the morphological analysis of the wordforms, so by including both singular and plural nouns in the same target set, a wrong analysis will not make any difference for the user, because the wordform is the same. The essive case has no number marker, and with this solution we were able to include the essive case in the activity.

For our new solution for the number ambiguity, we are generating the distractors for multiple-choice with an algorithm according to the analysis of the target word: the distractors will have the same number, but different case, as the target word. Essive can be distractor for both singular and plural. Only for target words in nominative case, which agree with the verb, the system might offer both the singular and the plural form. For the cloze-activity the system will accept both singular and plural forms if the target word has no agreement with the verbal, e.g. in example (4), as the object is accepted both *gándda* ("boy.Sg.Acc") and *gánddaid* ("boy.Pl.Acc").

4.2 Finding suitable texts

According to Meurers et al. (2011), the idea behind the VIEW approach is to allow the learner to choose up-to-date webpages on any topic they are interested in, because this clearly has a positive effect on learner motivation. Learners can use an ordinary search-engine interface to search for texts, or enter the URL of the page they want to enhance.

This is a good idea, but problematic for a minority language like North Saami. There are texts on the web, but the high rate of misspellings, 4% (Antonsen, 2013a), is problematic for getting reliable morphological analysis and disambiguation. Misspellings in AT-ICALL texts are also pedagogically problematic, since learners will be exposed to them.

Traditionally Saami speakers write in the majority language, and a native speaker's residence is decisive for the amount of schooling she has had in Saami, even if the situation has improved to some extent over the past 25 years. Still, native speakers are not exposed enough to the written language to be able to automate writing. According to research most L1 pupils both read and write better in majority language than Saami language (Helander, 2016, 15–16). Therefore Saami web-texts tend to be short, and with many misspellings.

There is a North Saami daily newspaper, but its web articles are behind a paywall. The Norwegian Saami broadcasting company (NRK-Sápmi) publishes a couple of new texts every day in North Saami, on topics which could be interesting for learners, but our analysis of 1.6 mill. words of these texts gives the rate of 5.7% misspellings, which is even higher than the average rate. That means that almost every sentence contains a misspelling. Also the texts published by the Finnish broadcasting company, YLE Sápmi, contain many misspellings.

Our solution is using texts from textbooks published on the web, and giving links to these texts as "recommended texts", see figure 3. In addition to news articles, NRK-Sápmi has published a collection of fairy tales, and they are willing to correct the texts on their site, if we proofread them. At this point it is not possible for the learners to choose up-to-date webpages on any topic they are interested in, because we have to ensure the quality of the spelling. There is a spell checker for North Saami, but it detects only non-word errors, and the correction suggestions are not chosen according to the context. An automatic spelling correction would not give the required quality.

Another way of getting around this problem has been to implement the possibility for teachers to upload proofread material or their own texts. They may then send the URL for each activity to their students.

4.3 Majority language in the texts

Even if there are good texts in North Saami on the web, they often contain fragments of the majority language (Norwegian, Finnish, Swedish), like a menu, or a dateline, as in example (2), with a dateline in Norwegian.

(2)   Publisert 19. jan. 2018 kl.   09:32
            Published 19. Jan. 2018 o'clock 09:32

We can remove the enhancement of elements which are specified in the HTML-code, like menus, but elements like datelines are not always specified. If none of the tokens are recognised as North Saami words, they do not constitute a problem for the ICALL-program. But this is something we have to keep an eye on, and it may require implementation of a language recogniser in the pipeline.

4.4 Handling variation

The orthography often allows variation in the spelling and the morphology. For example, the North Saami copula singular 3rd person indicative past tense has two normative orthographic forms, *lei* ~ *leai*. Also in other parts of the morphology there is much variation, e.g. the suffix for first person plural form of odd-stemmed verbs can, due to dialectal differences, be both *-it* and *-at*, like in *muitalit* ~ *muitalat* ("(we) tell"). The cloze-activity must accept all normative forms, and our solution is to generate the correct form(s) based on the analysis of the target word.

Also, we have solved the problem of non-normative forms in the same way. The descriptive analyser can to some extent recognise a word with non-normative spelling, but to get the key-answer to follow the normative spelling, the target form must be generated. In example (3), the verb *áiggon* ("(I) will") is spelled like it is pronounced in some dialects, and the analysis from the analyser is *áigut+V+TV+Ind+Prs+Sg1*. With these tags the normative form, *áiggun*, will be generated as the key answer for the cloze-activity, and the wordform *áiggon* will not be accepted as a correct answer.

(3)   ...ja mon áiggon   [áiggun] jearrat
           ...and I   will.Prs.Sg1 [will]   ask
           dus čiežanuppelohkái gažaldaga
           you seventeen   questions

The morphological and syntactic analysers for the ICALL-program are also used for the machine translation system described in Antonsen et al. (2017). This system is facing the same problem with non-normative forms in texts, and thus the work aimed at giving the descriptive analyser a better coverage for machine translation of North Saami web-texts, is also giving a better coverage to the analysis of web-texts for the ICALL-application.

4.5 Better feedback to the user

The VIEW system provides limited feedback to the user. In all the three activities where the user is asked to "do" something (click, choose, cloze), the answer turns red if it is wrong or green if it is correct. We have looked into how to give more sophisticated feedback to the user in the multiple-choice and cloze-activities. As suggested by Reynolds et al. (2014), one may give meaningful feedback based on the same NLP techniques as employed in the analysis, see figure 5.

```
"<De>"
    "de" Adv @ADVL>
"<boahtá>"
    "boahtit" V IV Ind Prs Sg3 @+FMAINV
"<stállu>"
    "stállu" N Sem/Hum Sg Nom @<SUBJ
"<ja>"
    "ja" CC @CVP
"<áigu>"
    "áigut" V IV Ind Prs Sg3 @+FAUXV
"<váldit>"
    "váldit" V TV Inf @-FMAINV
"<gándda>"
    "gánda" N Sem/Hum Sg Acc @<OBJ
"<.>"
    "." CLB
```

Figure 5: The FST and CG analysis of the sentence in example (4). The function tag for subject (SUBJ) is marked with an arrow towards the agreement verb, and both the object (OBJ) and adverbial (ADVL) are marked with an arrow towards the main verb (MAINV). The verb *váldit* has the analysis *váldit+V+TV+Inf* ("Verb+Transitive+Infinitive").

(4)   De   boahtá stállu   ja   áigu váldit
           Then comes the troll and will take
           .... (gánda)
           .... (the boy)

For many of the targets, it would be possible as a first feedback to an incorrect answer, to **highlight** in blue a word as a hint for choos-

De boahtá stállu ja áigu váldit   (gánda)

Figure 6: An example of highlighting a hint to the learner. The hint is the transitive verb *váldit*, which triggers the accusative case for the object, and the correct form is *gándda* ("boy.Sg.Acc"). The sentence is translated in example (4).

ing the correct form, like in figure 6, the verb *váldit* triggers the accusative case for the target word.

Usually the verb is the trigger for the case in the adverbial, moving towards a place (illative), or from a place (locative). For some of the oblique cases, the trigger will be a governing verb, like *ballat* ("to be afraid of") for locative or *liikot* ("to like") for illative. These verbs can be marked with an additional tag in the analysis, because the CG-grammar already contains sets of such verbs. For the nominative the hint is the verb agreeing with the noun.

For some of the non-finite verbforms, the trigger is an auxiliary verb, such as the copula for the perfect participle, e.g. in *lea borran* ("have eaten"). For infinitive the trigger may be an auxiliary (like *áiggun*) or a verb governing the infinitive (like *vikkan*): *áiggun borrat* ("(I) will eat") or *vikkan borrat* ("(I) try to eat"). The negation form of the main verb is preceded by the negation verb, inflected for person and number: *in bora* ("(I) don't eat"). Even though the negation form is a non-finite verb form, we considered it to be both important and difficult to learn to inflect correctly, especially for learners with a Germanic language as their first language, so we have included it as a target type of its own.

For the finite verb-form there is often a subject agreeing with the finite verb, but not always, since the subject may be omitted. But it seems that often it will be possible to identify and highlight a hint, and based on this, one might also generate a comment, like *"Look at the highlighted subject, the verb must agree"*. These are plans, and are not implemented yet.

5   User evaluation

We have identified two main user groups: teachers and learners. A group of teachers at an upper secondary school has started using the application and has given us some initial

feedback, which we have taken into account.

They suggested that it would be good to have additional information about the texts recommended by us. We added genre, length and difficulty level on each link to the texts.

Upon their request, we have removed the possibility to display key-answers from the exercises, since they were concerned that this feature might be used too much by the students, instead of trying to give the correct answer themselves. We also added information on how to convert PDF files into HTML (the format accepted by the application for file upload).

In addition to this, we asked both the students and the teacher at an introductory course in North Saami at a university to evaluate our application by replying to a targeted set of questions. They are still at the beginning of their course, but the teacher is confident that towards the end of the first semester the application will be useful and will provide exercises suitable to their level. In addition, the teacher says that is good for the students to train grammar in context, and read a variety of texts.

To the question about what should be improved, the teacher asks for more recommended texts. However, finding suitable texts for a minority language like North Saami is problematic (see 4.2).

We received feedback from three students using our application. All of the students are L2 speakers. Two of the three students have used at least two texts and at least three out of four of the activities proposed.

Two of the students declared that they had to struggle a bit before understanding how to use the application. In fact, one of the students noticed that it would be helpful to be able to use the same text for all topics. This confirms that, at least some of the users don't understand that it is possible to produce the desired exercise for each text. This means that we might rethink the layout of the application, but in order to do that it would be helpful to have more detailed feedback. One possibility to get a more explicit feedback might be to plan a short "usage session" with some users and get their instant opinions about the application, as was done by Bontogon et al. (2018).

Although the students like using the application to add variety to their study, two of them found the texts too difficult for their level of knowledge of the language.

In addition, a bug was reported, which caused the application not to show any correct/incorrect feedback when using the application together with a translation plugin. This has been fixed.

6 Conclusion

In this paper, we show that it is possible to adapt an ATICALL program like VIEW for North Saami. The analyser tools available are quite robust and with an acceptable F-score, but adapting and implementing the application for a minority language present some extra challenges.

The amount of variation in orthography made it necessary to generate the key-answer instead of using the original text. The same applied for misspellings. But the high rate of misspellings makes the analysis less reliable, and the ATICALL approach less pedagogical for learners, because they are exposed for the misspellings. Generating the key-answer makes it possible also to accept more morphological forms, and allows us to include also ambiguous target words.

It is also clear that although we provide the user with the feature of choosing any webpage, there are not enough suitable web-texts available of acceptable quality. The solution is thus to use proofread material, either as recommended web-texts or as teachers' uploaded texts. Still this ATICALL program was welcomed by students and teachers in both schools and universities, because of the sparseness of learning materials.

7 Future work

From the initial feedback received from students, we identified some problems with regards to the layout. In order to improve it and make it more user-friendly, we plan to organise a "usage session" with students to get instant opinions and comments about their experience with the application.

As described in 4.5, we plan to implement additional feedback, by highlighting hints in the sentence, if the learner writes or chooses an incorrect wordform. Based on the hint it would also be possible to generate comments for the learner.

We want to add adjectives as a target type. The inflection and derivation of adjectives is an important part of the grammar, and we are searching for suitable texts for this.

We have implemented three additional topics: identification of subject, object and adverbial. These are currently under testing, but we plan to have them in the stable version of our application soon, for both the highlight-activity and the click-activity. These additional topics will be relevant not only for language learners, but also for students following linguistic courses for North Saami as a native language.

We will concider implementation of a language recogniser in the pipeline, because there are often fragments of the majority language in the Saami webpages.

Acknowledgments

Thanks to Heli Uibo, who created the first implementation of VIEW for North Saami, which our work builds on. We also thank Ciprian Gerstenberger for technical support, and Trond Trosterud for useful discussions.

References

Lene Antonsen. 2013a. Čállinmeattáhusaid guorran. [English summary: Tracking misspellings]. *Sámi dieđalaš áigecála*, 2/2013:7–32.

Lene Antonsen. 2013b. Constraints in free-input question-answering drills. In *Proceedings of the second workshop on NLP for computer-assisted language learning (NoDaLiDa 2013)*, volume 17 of *Proceedings Series*, pages 11–26, Oslo. NEALT.

Lene Antonsen, Ciprian Gerstenberger, Maja Kappfjell, Sandra Nystø Rahka, Marja-Liisa Olthuis, Trond Trosterud, and Francis M. Tyers. 2017. Machine translation with North Saami as a pivot language. In *Proceedings of the 21st Nordic Conference of Computational Linguistics (NoDaLiDa 2017)*, volume 29 of *NEALT Proceedings Series*, pages 123–131, Linköping, Sweden. Linköping University Electronic Press.

Lene Antonsen, Ryan Johnson, Trond Trosterud, and Heli Uibo. 2013. Generating modular grammar exercises with finite-state transducers. In *Proceedings of the second workshop on NLP for computer-assisted language learning (NoDaLiDa*

2013), volume 17 of *NEALT Proceedings Series*, pages 27–38.

Lene Antonsen and Trond Trosterud. 2017. Ord sett innafra og utafra – en datalingvistisk analyse av nordsamisk. *Norsk lingvistisk tidsskrift*, 35(1):153–185.

Lene Antonsen, Trond Trosterud, and Linda Wiechetek. 2010. Reusing grammatical resources for new languages. In *Proceedings of the 7th International Conference on Language Resources and Evaluation (LREC 2010)*, pages 2782–2789, Stroudsburg. The Association for Computational Linguistics, ELRA.

Kenneth R. Beesley and Lauri Karttunen. 2003. *Finite State Morphology*. CSLI Studies in Computational Linguistics. CSLI publications, Stanford, USA.

Megan Bontogon, Antti Arppe, Lene Antonsen, Dorothy Thunder, and Jordan Lachler. 2018. Intelligent Computer Assisted Language Learning (ICALL) for nêhiyawêwin: An In-Depth User Experience Evaluation. *The Canadian Modern Languages Review*, 74(3).

Nils Øivind Helander. 2016. *Ohppojuvvon ja sohppojuvvon giella. Gielladidolašvuohta, čálamáhttu ja guovttegielatvuohta*. Diedut 1/2016. Sámi Allaskuvla, Guovdageaidnu.

Fred Karlsson. 1990. Constraint grammar as a framework for parsing running text. In *Papers Presented to the 13th International Conference on Computational Linguistics (COLING-90) on the Occasion of the 25th Anniversary of COLING and the 350th Anniversary of Helsinki University*, volume 3, Helsinki. Yliopistopaino.

Fred Karlsson, Atro Voutilainen, Juha Heikkilä, and Arto Anttila. 1995. *Constraint Grammar. A Language-Independent System for Parsing Unrestricted Text*. Mouton de Gruyter, Berlin – New York.

Detmar Meurers, Ramon Ziai, Luiz Amaral, Adriane Boyd, Aleksandar Dimitros, Vanessa Metcalf, and Niels Ott. 2011. Enhancing authentic web pages for language learners. In *Proceedings for the 5th Workshop on Innovative Use of NLP for Building Educational Applications (BEA-5) at NAACL-HLT 2010*, pages 10–18, Los Angeles.

Robert Reynolds, Eduard Schaf, and Detmar Meurers. 2014. A VIEW of Russian: Visual input enhancement and adaptive feedback. In *Proceedings of the third workshop on NLP for computer-assisted language learning at SLTC 2014, Uppsala University*, pages 98–112. Linköping Electronic Conference Proceedings.

Pekka Sammallahti. 1998. Saamic. In Daniel Abondolo, editor, *The Uralic Languages*, pages 43–96. Routledge, London.

Richard W. Schmidt. 1990. The role of consciousness in second language learning. *Applied Linguistics*, 11(2):129–158.

VISL-group. 2008. Constraint grammar. Documentation on internet. http://beta.visl.sdu.dk/constraint_grammar.html.

Normalization in Context: Inter-Annotator Agreement for Meaning-Based Target Hypothesis Annotation

Adriane Boyd
Department of Linguistics
University of Tübingen
`adriane@sfs.uni-tuebingen.de`

Abstract

We explore the contribution of explicit task contexts in the annotation of word-level and sentence-level normalizations for learner language. We present the annotation schemes and tools used to annotate both word- and sentence-level target hypotheses given an explicit task context for the Corpus of Reading Exercises in German (Ott et al., 2012) and discuss a range of inter-annotator agreement measures appropriate for evaluating target hypothesis and error annotation.

For learner answers to reading comprehension questions, we find that both the amount of task context and the correctness of the learner answer influence the inter-annotator agreement for word-level normalizations. For sentence-level normalizations, the teachers' detailed assessments of the learner answer meaning provided in the corpus give indications of the difficulty of the target hypothesis annotation task. We provide a thorough evaluation of inter-annotator agreement for multiple aspects of meaning-based target hypothesis annotation in context and explore measures beyond inter-annotator agreement that can potentially be used to evaluate the quality of normalization annotation.

1 Introduction

Learner language frequently contains non-canonical orthography and morphosyntactic constructions that present difficulties for natural language processing tools developed for standard language. Since manually annotated learner corpora are often small and the high degree of variation in learner productions leads to data sparsity issues even for larger learner corpora, it is useful to consider methods that normalize non-standard aspects of learner language. While normalization and applying standard language categories to learner language does not address the full spectrum of learner language analysis and fundamental concerns about analyzing learner language (cf. Meurers and Dickinson, 2017), it can facilitate access to learner language in applications such as corpus search tools and computer-aided language learning systems.

Normalizations such as the minimal target hypothesis from the Falko German learner corpus (Reznicek et al., 2012) have been developed in order to provide a version of a learner production that can be systematically searched and that is more appropriate for further manual or automatic analysis. The minimal target hypothesis contains a minimal number of modifications that convert the learner sentence into a locally grammatical sentence. As it may not be possible to determine exactly what the learner intended to say in an open-ended task such as an essay task, what constitutes a minimal change is based on grammatical properties, e.g., preserving a verb and modifying its arguments rather modifying the verb itself.

In terms of the difficulties an annotator may face while interpreting a learner utterance, consider the following learner utterance from the Hiroshima English Learners' Corpus (Miura, 1998):

(1) I don't know he live were.

It is possible to speculate about the intended meaning of this utterance, proposing multiple interpretations such as:

(2) a. I don't know if he was alive.

    b. I don't know where he lives.

Then consider (1) again within the task context: a translation task from Japanese into English of a sentence with the meaning *I don't know where he*

Adriane Boyd 2018. Normalization in context: Inter-annotator agreement for meaning-based target hypothesis annotation. *Proceedings of the 7th Workshop on NLP for Computer Assisted Language Learning at SLTC 2018 (NLP4CALL 2018)*. Linköping Electronic Conference Proceedings 152: 10–22.

lives. This task context makes it extremely likely that the intended meaning is that of (2b).

Without annotation guidelines based on detailed grammatical properties such as for Falko, target hypothesis annotation and likewise error annotation for learner language in open-ended tasks has been shown to be difficult to perform reliably (e.g., Fitzpatrick and Seegmiller, 2004; Lüdeling, 2008; Tetreault and Chodorow, 2008; Lee et al., 2009; Rosen et al., 2013; Dahlmeier et al., 2013). As an example, Dahlmeier et al. (2013) report Cohen's κ of 0.39 for the task of identifying which tokens should be edited in the NUCLE corpus of English student essays.

In contrast to open-ended tasks, a more explicit task context can provide more information about the potential meaning of a learner production (Meurers, 2015), thereby facilitating a more reliable interpretation of the form and meaning and thus more reliable annotation of target hypotheses, which preserve the intended meaning instead of prioritizing particular grammatical features. For the ComiGS corpus, which contains explicit task contexts in the form of comic strips used in picture description tasks, Köhn and Köhn (2018) report $\kappa = 0.86$ for the same task of identifying which tokens should be normalized.

In this paper, we systematically explore the dependence of normalization on task context through manual annotation studies, focusing on L2 learner responses in a reading comprehension task context. We explore inter-annotator agreement measures for normalization and error annotation, considering the use of related evaluation metrics beyond inter-annotator agreement for the direct evaluation of normalization annotation.

2 Background

Numerous manual annotation studies have shown that target hypothesis annotation is difficult to perform reliably, and since error annotation depends on the formulation of target hypotheses (cf. Hirschmann et al., 2007), inter-annotator agreement for error annotation has likewise had lower levels of reliability (e.g., Fitzpatrick and Seegmiller, 2004; Lüdeling, 2008; Tetreault and Chodorow, 2008; Lee et al., 2009; Rosen et al., 2013; Dahlmeier et al., 2013). For example, a detailed annotation study for the CzeSL corpus of L2 Czech shows a wide range of inter-annotator agreement results for the presence of different

types of error tags (Rosen et al., 2013), from $\kappa > 0.6$ for *incorrect stem*, *incorrect inflection*, and *incorrect word boundary* to $\kappa < 0.2$ for *ill-formed complex verb forms* and *incorrect pronominal references*. The authors perform a detailed inspection of the *agreement* errors ($\kappa = 0.54$) that reveals that half of the disagreements correspond to differing target hypotheses, where the annotators provided the correct error tags for their respective target hypotheses, but since these differ, the error annotation is inconsistent.

2.1 Task Context

For the contribution of available task context with respect to inter-annotator reliability, several studies on normalization annotation for in both L1 and L2 task contexts report promising results. In a native language setting, Lee et al. (2009) investigate annotators' judgments of article/number selections for English nouns in a sentence containing noun phrase gap. Annotators choose which noun article (*a/an*, *the*, no article) and number combinations (*singular*, *plural*) are possible in this context. For the five possible categories, Cohen's κ increases from $\kappa = 0.55$ to $\kappa = 0.60$ when the available context increases from the current sentence with the gap to include five preceding sentences. In addition, κ increases when the noun has already been mentioned in the context and for those article/number combinations that are much more frequent overall, e.g., the article/number combination *the sun* is much more frequent than all other article/number combinations involving *sun*, so annotators are more consistent about their decisions for *the sun* than less frequent combinations.

In an L2 setting, promising interannotator agreement results are reported for the ComiGS (Comic Strips Retold by Learners of German) corpus (Köhn and Köhn, 2018), an L2 German learner corpus where learners write descriptions of stories presented without accompanying text in comic strips. The corpus is manually annotated with minimal and extended target hypotheses largely following the Falko guidelines (Reznicek et al., 2012), and in contrast to previous studies of target hypothesis annotation in learner corpora, the ComiGS corpus includes an explicit context in which to interpret the learner productions. For the identification of which tokens need to be modified in the minimal target hypothesis in ComiGS, they report $\kappa = 0.856$ and for the extended target hypotheses $\kappa = 0.74$ (cf. $\kappa = 0.39$ for NUCLE (Dahlmeier et al., 2013), although clearly many differences between the annotation studies make a direct comparison difficult).

2.2 Inter-Annotator Agreement for Normalization Annotation

Evaluations of inter-annotator agreement for normalization annotation are typically performed for several perspectives on the manual annotation. As an example of some possible evaluations, the NUCLE corpus (Dahlmeier et al., 2013), which contains both normalizations and associated errors tags, presents inter-annotator agreement results for three aspects:

- **Normalization identification**: Do annotators agree on which tokens are normalized?

- **Error tag given norm. identification**: For those tokens where both annotators agree that a modification is needed, do they agree on the error tag assigned?

- **Error+norm. given norm. identification**: For those tokens where both annotators agree that a modification is needed, do they agree on both the error tag and the normalization?

As an alternative to examining only those cases where both annotators agree that a modification is necessary, which excludes many potentially interesting cases where annotators disagree about whether to make a modification in the first place, the CzeSL inter-annotator agreement evaluation (Rosen et al., 2013) considers each error tag separately as a binary annotation task:

- **Error tag identification**: For a given error category, do annotators agree on which tokens are annotated with this category?

Both Dahlmeier et al. (2013) and Rosen et al. (2013) report the agreement coefficient Cohen's κ (Cohen, 1960), which measures agreement for categorical annotation tasks for two annotators. Cohen's κ (Cohen, 1960) and Krippendorff's α (Krippendorff, 1980) are frequently used inter-annotator agreement measures for evaluating binary or categorical annotation decisions, e.g., *Is a token modified?* or *Is a token annotated with category X?*. Inter-annotator agreement measures estimate how likely it is that annotators agreed (for κ)

or disagreed (for α) by chance and calculate the degree of agreement beyond the level expected by chance alone.

The values for both Cohen's κ and Krippendorff's α range from -1 (perfect disagreement) to 1 (perfect agreement) with 0 as chance agreement only. Cohen's κ is limited to nominal categories (all disagreements are counted equally) and only two annotators, while Krippendorff's α has the advantages that three or more annotators can be included and that not only nominal categories but also annotations on ordinal or interval scales or with sets of categorical tags can be compared more precisely. See Artstein and Poesio (2009) for a detailed overview of inter-annotator agreement for linguistic annotation.

As explored in Bollmann et al. (2016), Cohen's κ, Krippendorff's α, and other related measures of agreement are not appropriate for use with normalization annotation itself, as in the NUCLE evaluation of **error+norm. given norm. identification**. The difficulties lie in the fact that the possible values for normalizations are not a small, finite set of categories but the set of all possible tokens in the target language. Given a relatively small annotated corpus, it is not possible to estimate how likely a given token might be in order to estimate chance agreement and even if it were possible, it would still not take into account the fact that a target hypothesis is frequently a form closely related to the original token. Additionally, κ and α give a higher weight to less frequent annotations, which means that normalizations for infrequent words play a larger role in the agreement coefficient even though an annotator's performance typically does not depend directly on the frequency of the word to be normalized. In fact, the opposite is often true: a misspelled rare name provided in the task context may be simple to normalize while a frequent determiner may be more challenging.

As there is no consensus on suitable agreement measures for normalization or target hypothesis annotation, we will primarily report percentage agreement in the following studies. We return to the issue of inter-annotator agreement measures for full target hypotheses in section 4.2.4.

3 Data

The normalization annotation experiments presented in the next section are performed using the

Q: Was sah der Mann, als er die Tür aufmachte?
'What did the man see when he opened the door?'

SA: Er sahe seiner Frau.
'He saw his wife.'

TA: Als er die Tür aufmachte, sah der Mann seine Frau.
'When he opened the door, the man saw his wife.'

RT: Als er die Tür aufmachte (sie weinte dabei, die Tür), sahen ihm die blaßblauen Augen seiner Frau entgegn.
'When he opened the door (it creaked, the door), his wife's pale blue eyes awaited him.'

MA1: Binary: *appropriate*, Detailed: *correct*

MA2: Binary: *appropriate*, Detailed: *correct*

Figure 1: CREG Example

Corpus of Reading Exercises in German (CREG, Ott et al., 2012), a German L2 learner corpus containing learner answers to reading comprehension exercises, which was collected in to enable research into learner language in a task-based context. The learners are students in German classes at two American universities who completed reading comprehension exercises as part of their coursework. The corpus contains: 1) reading texts, 2) comprehension questions, 3) teacher-provided target answer(s), 4) student answers to the questions, and 5) teacher assessments of the student answer meaning.

An example student answer (SA) to a comprehension question (Q) is shown in Figure 1 along with the target answer (TA) provided by a teacher and an excerpt from the reading text (RT). The meaning of each student answer is assessed by two teachers (MA1/2), who provide a binary assessment of the meaning (*appropriate* or *inappropriate* as an answer to the question) without taking spelling or grammar into account and a detailed classification of how the student answer differs from the provided target answer using the categories: *correct*, *missing concept*, *extra concept*, *blend*, and *non-answer*. Student answers marked as *appropriate* in the binary assessment are most frequently *correct* in the detailed assessment, but *appropriate* answers may also contain missing concepts, extra concepts, or blends.

Our experiments will primarily use data from CREG-5K, a subcorpus of CREG that contains

Binary Detailed	Approp. (%)	Inapprop. (%)
Correct	76.9	0.0
Missing Concept	14.5	43.7
Extra Concept	6.2	3.2
Blend	2.4	50.2
Non-Answer	0.0	2.9

Table 1: Meaning Assessments in CREG-5K

~5000 student answers with a balanced number of appropriate and inappropriate answers. In total, CREG-5K contains 5138 student answers to 877 questions for 98 reading texts. The reading texts vary greatly in length, with an average of 961 tokens and a standard deviation of 1271 tokens. The student answers have been selected to contain a minimum of four tokens and have an average length of 11.75 tokens with a standard deviation of 7.13 tokens. The distribution of binary and detailed meaning assessments for CREG-5K is shown in Figure 1.

4 Experiments

On the basis of the CREG corpus, we explore the extent to which *context* and *appropriateness* play a role in the normalization of learner language. We first perform two normalization annotation studies on non-words in CREG-5K. Our goal is to investigate whether the amount of task context plays a role in inter-annotator agreement and whether appropriate answers can be more reliably normalized than inappropriate ones. Next, in section 4.2 we will describe the annotation of full meaning-based target hypotheses for the appropriate answers in CREG-5K and explore the evaluation of inter-annotator agreement for full normalizations and error tags.

4.1 Non-Word Normalization

We focus initially on non-word normalization, which allows us to sample a range of cases across the corpus from typos to English translations provided within student answers. The texts are automatically tokenized using the OpenNLP tokenizer trained on the non-headline sections of TüBa-D/Z version 9.0 (Telljohann et al., 2004) and non-words are identified automatically for the annotators. A *non-word* is defined as a token that does not appear in the question or reading text (if available in the experimental condition) or in the

DeReWo list of the 100,000 most frequent inflected words in a large German reference corpus
(Institut für Deutsche Sprache, 2009).[1]

In two related experiments, we investigate the
roles of task context and answer appropriateness
in non-word normalization. We hypothesize that it
is easier to perform non-word normalization reliably given more task context and that appropriate
answers are easier to normalize than inappropriate
ones, since annotators know the intended meaning of an appropriate answer from the task context.
We first describe the annotation scheme and annotation tool used in both experiments, then present
the experimental results.

4.1.1 Non-Word: Annotation Scheme

Non-words are annotated with a normalization
that would be part of a form-meaning target hypothesis (a target hypothesis that preserves the intended meaning of the student answer while taking the task context into account, see section 4.2)
for the student's answer given the available task
context. Each non-word is additionally annotated
with the amount of context required for the annotator to be confident that the provided normalization is the intended token in this context. If the
annotator cannot be confident of a single normalization, multiple normalizations can be provided
along with the context category *Hard*. The annotators are instructed to consider each context category in order:

- Real Word: non-word is a real word
- No Context: umlaut spellings with *e*, *ss* vs. *ß*
- Answer: the student answer alone
- Question + Answer: the answer along with
  the question
- Reading Text + Question + Answer: the full
  task context
- Hard (ambiguous, English): a single normal-
  ization cannot be chosen with confidence

When the full context is not available (only in
some conditions in Experiment 1), only the context categories for the provided context should be
annotated.

---

[1]This process misses some non-words and misspellings
in the corpus because the DeReWo word list contains both
old and new German spellings and also some proper names
such as *Fisher* that cause our automatic selection process to
miss some tokens in CREG that require a word-level normalization. All non-word normalizations are reviewed and
additional non-word annotations are added in the full form-
meaning target hypotheses in section 4.2.

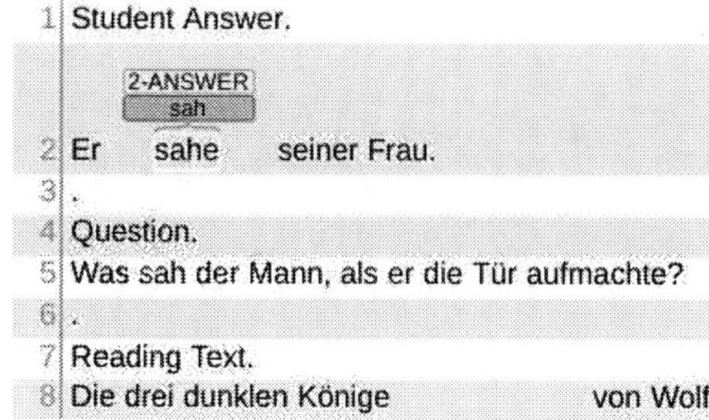

Figure 2: Non-Word Annotation in WebAnno

4.1.2 Non-Word: Annotation Tool

The non-words were annotated using custom layers in the tool WebAnno (Yimam et al., 2014). The
student answers were preprocessed using a UIMA
pipeline in order to tokenize them, identify non-
words, and insert empty annotation spans to be
filled in by the annotators. A screenshot of the WebAnno annotation environment is shown in Figure 2 for the student answer *Er sahe seiner Frau.*
'He saw his wife.' in response to the question *Was
sah der Mann, als er die Tür aufmachte?* 'What
did the man see as he opened the door?' The annotator has annotated the non-word *sahe* with the
normalization *sah* 'saw' and specified the required
context as the student answer alone.

4.1.3 Non-Word Experiment 1: Context

To evaluate the role of context in non-word normalization, the correct answers from CREG-5K
(binary assessment: *appropriate*) were annotated.
There were 1152 potential non-words in 2574 answers to 877 questions about 98 reading texts. The
non-words were divided into four conditions by
reading text, so that a reading text and its associated questions/answer are only included in one
condition:

- training (10%)
- answer context only (15%)
- answer + question (15%)
- answer + question + reading text (60%)

Since we intend to annotate all non-words given
the full context for the full form-meaning target
hypotheses (see section 4.2), the non-words are
not distributed equally between the conditions in
order to reduce the reannotation burden in the next
stage.

Two annotators annotated the training instances
(10%) and met to discuss disagreements and to re-

	Norm.	Context	
	%	# Cats	α
Answer	74.8	4	0.696
A + Question	79.0	5	0.689
A + Q + Text	83.8	6	0.602

Table 2: IAA for Non-Words: Context

	W	N	A	Q	R	H	Σ
W	41	0	26	1	2	2	72
N	0	71	4	0	1	3	79
A	5	8	321	4	7	18	363
Q	0	0	13	11	0	0	24
R	0	0	26	1	9	1	37
H	0	0	6	0	1	6	13
Σ	46	79	396	17	20	30	588

Table 3: Confusion Matrix: Non-Word with Full Context

	Norm.	Context
	%	α
Appropriate	83.3	0.678
Inappropriate	78.6	0.588

Table 4: IAA for Non-Words: Appropriateness

fine the annotation guidelines, then annotated the remaining instances (90%) independently. The results are shown in Table 2. As discussed in section 2.2, the agreement for the normalizations is presented as percentage agreement on the exact form provided and the agreement for the context category using Krippendorff's α.

As a result of the fact that the number of categories is not identical across conditions, the α values cannot be compared directly, however indicate moderate to substantial agreement on the context tags. When only the student answer is available, annotators agree 74.8% of the time on the normalization. This increases to 79.0% if the question is also available and to 83.8% if the question and reading text[2] are provided, showing that the presence of an explicit task context does enable a higher degree of reliability in normalization annotation.

For the annotations with the full context (60%, all six context tags are included), the confusion matrix for the context tags is shown in Figure 3. Some frequent sources of disagreement are rare inflections such as second person plural subjunctive forms (e.g., *stehet* 'would stand'), where one annotator annotated them as *Real Word* and the other normalized them to more frequent third person singular indicative forms (*steht* 'stand') with the category *Answer*, and instances where there are multiple, acceptable alternatives for prepositions in a particular context and one annotator consistently provided more alternatives, annotating such cases as *Hard* (vs. *Answer* for the other annotator).

4.1.4 Non-Word Experiment 2: Appropriateness

In the second non-word normalization experiment, the role of *appropriateness* is considered. The non-words consist of 529 non-words in 365 answers, presented to the annotator with the

full reading text context. Since the appropriate answers from CREG-5K were annotated in the previous experiment, the appropriate answers come from CREG-1032 and other CREG subcorpora, while the inappropriate answers come from CREG-1032 and CREG-5K.

The two annotators from the previous experiment completed the annotation independently without any further training. The results are shown in Table 4. When the answer meaning has been assessed as *appropriate*, annotators agree on a single normalization in 83.3% of instances, nearly 5% higher than when the answer is *inappropriate*. Krippendorff's α, which is now comparable across both conditions since all six categories were used, is 0.678 for appropriate answers and drops to 0.588 for inappropriate answers, showing that annotators are more reliable in terms of the contribution of the task context for appropriate answers. This may be due to the fact that incorrect answers may include additional information that is not present in any part of the task context, so it may be more difficult to choose a context annotation.

4.2 Form-Meaning Target Hypothesis Annotation

Moving from non-word annotation to full target hypothesis annotation for the complete student answers, we present pilot results for the annotation of *form-meaning target hypotheses* on the *appropriate* answers from CREG-5K, the same subset of

---

[2]As the students answering the reading comprehension questions do not have access to the teacher target answers while responding, the target answers are not presented to the annotations as part of this experiment.

CREG annotated in Experiment 1 (section 4.1.3) containing 2574 student answers.

A *form-meaning target hypothesis* (FMTH) is defined as a target hypothesis that provides a grammatical version of the student answer that:

- preserves as much of the meaning of the answer as possible

- respects the task context

If normalizations are necessary, these modifications should be as minimal as possible and align as closely as possible with material from the target answer, the question, and the reading text, e.g., if there is a missing concept, the inserted tokens should come directly from the task context.

After completing the non-word annotation experiments, one annotator reannotated the subset of non-words from Experiment 1 not presented in the full task context (30%) and the data was converted to Prague Markup Language[3] in preparation for use with the tool *feat* (see section 4.2.2). This annotator and a new second annotator performed the full target hypothesis and error annotation presented in the following sections.

4.2.1 FMTH: Error Annotation Scheme

The focus of the form-meaning target hypothesis annotation is on the normalization itself, however error annotation is also included to encourage a careful, reliable analysis of the student answers during the annotation process. The error annotation scheme attempts to parallel the CzeSL annotation scheme where possible, with non-words normalized in the first layer of annotation (word) and the full sentence normalized in the second layer of annotation (sentence). The top-level categories of the annotation scheme are presented in Table 5. For each error category, the table specifies whether a tag is possible on the word or sentence layers.

The top half of the table shows error tags similar to CzeSL, which are typical types of error tags seen in error-annotated learner corpora, and the bottom half of the table introduces new tags specific to the annotation of target hypotheses within a provided task context. In some instances, normalizations are necessary because of the question or reading text content, e.g., the tense of a student answer needs to be adjusted (tag: *Question*) or a proper name from the reading text is misspelled (tag: *Reading Text*). Students may have

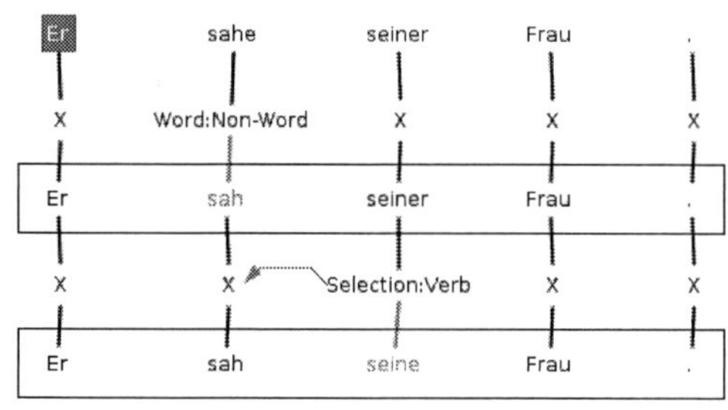

Figure 3: feat Annotation Tool

copied material from the reading text in a problematic way (e.g., copied 'not only' without the corresponding 'but also', *Copied - Problematic*), provided an answer that has a slightly incorrect meaning (*Answer Meaning*), or provided extra concepts that the annotators cannot normalize as consistently as material based on the task context (*Extraneous*). Problematic cases are discussed in further detail in section 4.2.3.

4.2.2 FMTH: Annotation Tool

The form-meaning target hypothesis annotation is performed using the tool *feat* (Flexible Error Annotation Tool), which was developed as part of the CzeSL project (Hana et al., 2012). We extend *feat* to support the CREG FMTH error scheme and to enable annotators to search for strings within long reading texts in order to make it easier to find the relevant sections and copied material.[4]

A screenshot of the *feat* annotation for the example from Figure 1 is shown in Figure 3. The top layer of tokens shows the original tokenized text, the middle layer shows the non-word normalizations, and the bottom layer shows the full form-meaning target hypothesis. In this example, the verb *sah* 'saw' selects the accusative case, so *seiner* 'his (DAT/GEN)' is normalized to *seine* 'his (NOM/ACC)' and the corresponding error tag *Selection:Verb* is chosen with a pointer identifying the head that selects this token.

4.2.3 Difficult Cases

Annotators encountered a range of difficult cases while annotating form-meaning target hypotheses, which relate to the nature of certain types of reading comprehension questions and aspects of annotating given a context provided by a written text.

Error Category	Word	Sent.	Description
Word	✓	✓	Capitalization, stem/inflection, word boundary, non-word error
Lexicon/Style	✓	✓	For lexical choice or style reasons the original token cannot be integrated into the target hypothesis
Selection		✓	Error in syntactic selection
Agreement		✓	Error in agreement
Order		✓	Error in word order
Modifier		✓	Error in a genitive modifier
Negation		✓	*kein* vs. *nicht*, double negatives, negative polarity items
Typo - POS		✓	Small spelling differences of 1-2 letters resulting in a different POS where a typo is more likely than a linguistically-motivated error
Secondary		✓	Annotator's normalizations require subsequent modifications to the student answer
Problem/Other	✓	✓	Problematic cases
Question	✓	✓	Target hypothesis chosen depends on the question content (providing a standalone answers, verb tense)
Reading Text	✓	✓	Target hypothesis chosen depends on the reading text content
Copied - Problematic		✓	Material lifted from the reading text that is not grammatical in the answer context
Answer Meaning		✓	Answer meaning does not correspond to target answer(s)
Extraneous		✓	Extra concepts in student answers

Table 5: Top-Level Categories in CREG FMTH Error Annotation Scheme

Q: Nennen Sie zwei Zimmer im Erdgeschoss.
'Name two rooms on the ground floor.'

SA: ein Wohnzimmer und ein Badzimmer
'a living room and a bathroom'

TA: Im Erdgeschoss gibt es ein Bad, Gäste WC, eine Küche und ein Wohn/Esszimmer.
'On the ground floor there is a bathroom, a guest bathroom, a kitchen, and a living/dining room.'

Figure 4: Difficult Cases: Enumerated Answers

Enumerated answers Enumerated answers present a particular problem for the reading comprehension task scenario. An example of a question with an enumerated answer is shown in Figure 4. When creating the CREG corpus, Ott et al. (2012) noticed a larger degree of disagreement in meaning assessment for enumerated answers, which appears to be due to the fact that is unclear how complete an enumeration needs to be to consider a student answer *appropriate*.

The target answers typically provide an exhaustive list of all items while an appropriate student answer provides only the number requested in the question. For form-meaning target hypothesis annotation, the annotators cannot rely on the target answers when evaluting the meaning of the student answer and when concepts are missing, there is also not a clear choice for which concept to insert into the student answer.

Extra concepts Students occasionally provide material in their responses that comes from their own world knowledge rather than the reading text. Figure 5 shows one instance where the student provides additional facts in an answer, which an annotator cannot evaluate within the task context.

Problematic copied material There are complicated annotation decisions to be made when the student has lifted material from the reading text in a problematic way. A few unnecessary words may be concatenated onto the end of a correct response or one half of a correlative conjunction pair may be missing. Such a case is shown in Figure 6, where the student has copied 'not only' from a sentence in the reading text without copying 'but also'. It is difficult for an annotator to decide whether to delete the first half of the correlative pair or insert the remainder of the sentence from the reading text, since neither choice would affect the meaning

Proceedings of the 7th Workshop on NLP for Computer Assisted Language Learning at SLTC 2018 (NLP4CALL 2018)

Q: Wo leben die meisten Amischen heute?
'Where do most Amish live today?'

TA: Heute leben die meisten Amischen in Ohio, Pennsylvanien und Indiana.
'Today most Amish live in Ohio, Pennsylvania, and Indiana.'

SA: Die meisten Amischen leben in Ohio, Pennsylvania, und Indiana. Es gibt auch ein paar in Yoder, Kansas.
'Most Amish live in Ohio, Pennsylvania, and Indiana. There are also a few in Yoder, Kansas.'

MA: Binary: *appropriate*, Detailed: *extra concept*

Figure 5: Difficult Cases: Extra Concepts

Q: Was tat Herr Muschler, als seine Frau mit ihm zu sprechen versuchte?
'What was Herr Muschler doing while his wife was trying to talk to him?'

SA: Er sah nicht nur fern und die Zietung.
'He not only watched TV and the newspaper.'

TA: Er sah fern, las die Zeitung, rauchte eine Zigarette und trank ein Glas Bier.
'He watched TV, read the newspaper, smoked a cigarette, and drank a glass of beer.'

RT: Herr Muschler sah nicht nur fern, sondern las außerdem noch die Zeitung.
'He was not only watching TV but also reading the newspaper.'

MA1: Binary: *appropriate*, Detailed: *extra concept*

MA2: Binary: *appropriate*, Detailed: *missing concept*

Figure 6: Difficult Cases: Problematic Copied Material

assessment for the response.

Reading text interpretation The least resolvable issues arise when two annotators disagree on the interpretation of the reading text itself. In Figure 7, the subject of an interview in a reading text states that he was unsure how many people might come to a demonstration and the student answer mentions 'force against not too many people', which potentially needs to be normalized under *Answer Meaning* to align with the target answer. One annotator interpreted the text to mean that the organizer was worried that not enough people would come and the other annotator thought that he was worried that too many people would come.

Q: Warum hatte Schorlemmer zu Beginn Angst?
'Why was Schorlemmer afraid at the beginning?'

TA: Er wusste nicht, wie viele Menschen kommen würden und ob die Polizei mit Gewalt gegen die Demonstration vorgeht.
'He did not know how many people would come and if the police would respond to the demonstration with force.'

SA: dass die Polizei mit Gewalt gegen nicht zu viele Menschen kommen
'that the police would come with force against not too many people'

RT: Ich hatte noch große Angst. Zum einen, weil ich nicht wusste, wie viele Menschen kommen würden. Zum anderen, weil ich Angst hatte, dass die Polizei mit Gewalt gegen die Demonstration vorgehen würde.
'I was still very scared. On the one hand, because I didn't know how many people would come. On the other hand, because I was scared that the police would respond to the demonstration with force.'

MA1: Binary: *appropriate*, Detailed: *correct*

MA2: Binary: *appropriate*, Detailed: *missing concept*

Figure 7: Difficult Cases: Reading Text Interpretation

With differing interpretations of the reading text, there is little hope for similar target hypotheses. Despite the explicit task context, such ambiguous statements may still be present in a reading text and lead to inter-annotator disagreement.

4.2.4 IAA for Meaning-Based Target Hypotheses

After annotating approximately 75% of the CREG-5K appropriate answers with meaning-based target hypotheses in a collaborative process including many discussions of difficult cases and refinements to the annotation manual, the two annotators annotated a subcorpus of 250 student answers independently in order to evaluate inter-annotator agreement. The subcorpus contains 3259 tokens in 250 appropriate student answers that have been sampled randomly from CREG-5K.

In order for our evaluation to be comparable to the evaluation of similar L2 German target hypotheses in Köhn and Köhn (2018), annotations on the word and sentence level are aligned with the original tokens by merging any inserted tokens into the annotation for the following token, with annotations at the end of a sentence merged into the preceding token. In case there are multiple error tags on a single token or in merged annotations, these are treated as a set of error tags on the original token.

Cohen's κ[5] for **normalization identification** (see section 2.2 for detailed descriptions) is 0.68, which shows substantial agreement and falls in between results reported for NUCLE ($\kappa = 0.39$) and for ComiGS ($\kappa = 0.86$). For **error tag given normalization**, κ is 0.47, which is slightly lower than NUCLE ($\kappa = 0.55$) for a relatively similar set of error tags. However, our annotation allows annotators to annotate multiple error tags on a single word, resulting in 57 combinations of error tags (for 15 individual tags) which are treated as separate tags in κ's comparisons. Using the more appropriate MASI distance metric for set annotations (Passonneau, 2006), we obtain $\alpha_{MASI} = 0.50$ for 15 error tags, again given that both annotators normalized the token.

We find only small differences between **error tag given normalization** ($\kappa = 0.47$), which ignores cases where only one annotator annotated an error, and simply **error tag** for all tokens, with $\kappa = 0.45$. Although ~86% of the tokens are not annotated with error tags, chance-corrected agreement measures account for the high probability that an original token remains unmodified in a target hypothesis and that most tokens in the corpus are not annotated with error tags.

As with non-word normalizations, we calculate only the percentage agreement for the normalizations themselves. For cases where both annotators agreed that a token should be normalized, the same normalization is provided in 70% of instances. Given the fact that target hypothesis annotation can involve complicated edits and reordering, it is not surprising that the agreement is slightly lower than in the non-word experiments reported Table 2 and Table 4.

We perform a similar analysis of **error tag identification** to compare our results to those reported for CzeSL in Rosen et al. (2013). For the top-level error tags that appear at least ten times in our subcorpus, we evaluate whether annotators agreed about which tokens are annotated with a particular tag. These results are shown in Table 6. As in CzeSL, there is a wide range of agreement

Error Tag	κ	Avg. Tags / Annotator
Punctuation	0.65	58
Order	0.57	42
Selection	0.46	171
Typo	0.40	5
Agreement	0.38	60
Word	0.36	17
Lexicon	0.18	43
Secondary	0.17	24
Question	0.15	43
Reading Text	0.07	38
Answer Meaning	0.03	25

Table 6: IAA for Error Tag Identification

with some error tags being annotated fairly reliably (Punctuation, Order) and others with little agreement beyond chance (Reading Text, Answer Meaning).

A common thread in the inspection of difficult cases throughout the annotation process is that difficulties frequently occur when the detailed meaning assessment is not *correct* for one or both teacher assessments. Since an answer with a *missing concept*, *extra concept*, or *blend* either does not supply the correct answer meaning or may include material from outside the task context, this is not surprising. To explore the relationship between difficulty as perceived by the annotators and inter-annotator agreement, we consider three partitions of the data: 1) both detailed meaning assessment are correct vs. all other combinations of assessments, 2) the two detailed meaning assessments are identical vs. different, and 3) the cases where at least one detailed assessment includes a particular detailed tag.

We calculate κ for **normalization identification**, κ for **error tag** for all error tags as shown in Table 7. Agreement measures for both drop slightly for *correct* vs. *other* but surprisingly increase slightly for answers where the teachers did not agree on the detailed assessment. Larger differences are seen for the individual detailed categories, with *blend* and *extra concept* instances showing much lower agreement, in particular for error tags related to *extra concepts*. In general, κ for **normalization identification** does not appear to reflect annotators' perception of overall difficulty, which can be explained by the fact that merely identifying problematic spans is only a

---

[5]All inter-annotator agreement measures are calculated using the scripts by Thomas Lippincott and Rebecca Passonneau: `https://cswww.essex.ac.uk/Research/nle/arrau/Lippincott/agreement.tgz`

	All	**Both Correct**	**Other**	**MA1 = MA2**	**MA1 $\neq$ MA2**	**MA Includes**			
						Correct	**Blend**	**Missing**	**Extra**
# Tokens	3259	2143	1116	2340	919	2914	157	652	455
# Answers	250	175	75	193	57	225	9	49	24
κ, Norm. Id.	0.68	0.69	0.66	0.68	0.70	0.69	0.60	0.70	0.62
κ, Error Tag	0.45	0.47	0.42	0.45	0.46	0.47	0.43	0.49	0.29
CharacTER	0.11	0.10	0.13	0.11	0.10	0.10	0.12	0.12	0.14

Table 7: IAA by Detailed Meaning Assessment

small part of the annotation task.

Since none of the inter-annotator agreement measures are suitable for comparing agreement between the normalization annotation, we turn to alternate metrics that have been proposed for the related tasks of machine translation evaluation and paraphrase detection. These metrics should ideally provide a more holistic evaluation of whether two target hypotheses are similar to each other on the sentence level rather than focusing on annotations for individual tokens. One recent metric from machine translation evaluation, CharacTER, seems particularly promising since it has been shown to correlate highly with human judgments for languages with richer morphology such as German and Russian (Wang et al., 2016).

CharacTER is adapted from the *translation edit rate* metric (TER, Olive, 2005), which calculates the number of edits required to convert one translation to a reference translation on the word level. CharacTER extends this to consider both *shifts* on the word level to align two sentences (counted as the average number of characters in the words shifted) and then further *character edits* required to transform the shifted sentence into the reference translation. This combination allows for variations in word order and small differences in morphological endings to be counted in a more fine-grained way than word-only edits. CharacTER is formally defined as:

$$\text{CharacTER} = \frac{\text{shift cost + edit distance}}{\text{\# characters in the hypothesis sentence}}$$

The CharacTER score is lower when two sentences are more similar, with a score of 0 for identical sentences. Since it is intended to compare a system translation to a reference translation, we extend CharacTER[6] to calculate scores with each annotator providing the reference translation once and average these scores on the sentence level. Although a translation metric does not account for

the overlap between the original student answer and the target hypothesis (thus such low overall scores when compared to machine translation), the types of cases that teachers found difficult to assess and that annotators found difficult to normalize are reflected more accurately (with higher CharacTER scores) than with other measures.

5 Conclusion / Outlook

In experiments on word-level and sentence-level normalization for an L2 German reading comprehension corpus, we show that inter-annotator agreement for normalization annotation increases when more of the task context is provided to the annotators and that *appropriate* answers can be normalized more reliably than inappropriate answers. In the evaluation of inter-annotator agreement for full form-meaning target hypotheses, which preserve the intended meaning while taking the task context into account, we explore a range of inter-annotator agreement metrics and how the CharacTER machine translation metric shows promise for the comparison of normalization annotations on the sentence level.

In future work on evaluating inter-annotator agreement for normalization annotation, we would like to explore the use of additional machine translation metrics and related metrics from paraphrase detection and plagiarism detection, since these could potentially capture many of the similarities in form and meaning while accounting for the fact that annotators' normalizations should come from the provided context as much as possible.

Acknowledgments

We would like to thank the anonymous reviewers for their helpful feedback. This work was supported by the German Research Foundation (DFG) under project ME 1447/2-1 and through the Collaborative Research Center 833.

---

[6] https://github.com/rwth-i6/CharacTER/

References

Ron Artstein and Massimo Poesio. 2009. Survey article: Inter-coder agreement for computational linguistics. *Computational Linguistics*, 34(4):1–42.

Marcel Bollmann, Stefanie Dipper, and Florian Petran. 2016. Evaluating inter-annotator agreement on historical spelling normalization. *Proceedings of LAW X – The 10th Linguistic Annotation Workshop*, pages 89–98.

Jacob Cohen. 1960. A coefficient of agreement for nominal scales. *Educational and Psychological Measurement*, 20(1):37–46.

Daniel Dahlmeier, Hwee Tou Ng, and Siew Mei Wu. 2013. Building a large annotated corpus of learner English: The NUS corpus of learner English. In *Proceedings of the Eighth Workshop on Innovative Use of NLP for Building Educational Applications*, pages 22–31. Association for Computational Linguistics.

Eileen Fitzpatrick and M. S. Seegmiller. 2004. The Montclair electronic language database project. In U. Connor and T.A. Upton, editors, *Applied Corpus Linguistics: A Multidimensional Perspective*. Rodopi, Amsterdam.

Jirka Hana, Alexandr Rosen, Barbora Štindlová, and Petr Jäger. 2012. Building a learner corpus. In *Proceedings of the Eight International Conference on Language Resources and Evaluation (LREC'12)*, Istanbul, Turkey. European Language Resources Association (ELRA).

Hagen Hirschmann, Seanna Doolittle, and Anke Lüdeling. 2007. Syntactic annotation of non-canonical linguistic structures. In *Proceedings of Corpus Linguistics 2007*, Birmingham.

Institut für Deutsche Sprache. 2009. Korpusbasierte Wortformenliste DEREWO, v-100000t-2009-04-30-0.1, mit Benutzerdokumentation. Technical Report IDS-KL-2009-02, Institut für Deutsche Sprache, Programmbereich Korpuslinguistik.

Christine Köhn and Arne Köhn. 2018. An annotated corpus of picture stories retold by language learners. In *Proceedings of the Joint Workshop on Linguistic Annotation, Multiword Expressions and Constructions (LAW-MWE-CxG-2018)*, pages 121–132. Association for Computational Linguistics.

Klaus Krippendorff. 1980. *Content Analysis: An Introduction to its Methodology*. Sage Publications, Beverly Hills, CA.

John Lee, Joel Tetreault, and Martin Chodorow. 2009. Human evaluation of article and noun number usage: Influences of context and construction variability. In *ACL 2009 Proceedings of the Linguistic Annotation Workshop III (LAW3)*. Association for Computational Linguistics.

Anke Lüdeling. 2008. Mehrdeutigkeiten und Kategorisierung: Probleme bei der Annotation von Lernerkorpora. In Maik Walter and Patrick Grommes, editors, *Fortgeschrittene Lernervarietäten: Korpuslinguistik und Zweispracherwerbsforschung*, pages 119–140. Max Niemeyer Verlag, Tübingen.

Detmar Meurers. 2015. Learner corpora and natural language processing. In Sylviane Granger, Gaëtanelle Gilquin, and Fanny Meunier, editors, *The Cambridge Handbook of Learner Corpus Research*, pages 537–566. Cambridge University Press.

Detmar Meurers and Markus Dickinson. 2017. Evidence and interpretation in language learning research: Opportunities for collaboration with computational linguistics. *Language Learning, Special Issue on Language learning research at the intersection of experimental, corpus-based and computational methods: Evidence and interpretation*. To appear.

Shogo Miura. 1998. Hiroshima English Learners' Corpus: English learner No. 2 (English I & English II). Department of English Language Education, Hiroshima University. http://purl.org/icall/helc.

Joseph Olive. 2005. Global autonomous language exploitation (gale). Technical report, DARPA/IPTO Proposer Information Pamphlet.

Niels Ott, Ramon Ziai, and Detmar Meurers. 2012. Creation and analysis of a reading comprehension exercise corpus: Towards evaluating meaning in context. In Thomas Schmidt and Kai Wörner, editors, *Multilingual Corpora and Multilingual Corpus Analysis*, Hamburg Studies in Multilingualism (HSM), pages 47–69. Benjamins, Amsterdam.

Rebecca Passonneau. 2006. Measuring agreement on set-valued items (MASI) for semantic and pragmatic annotation. In *Proceedings of the Fifth International Conference on Language Resources and Evauation (LREC-06)*.

Marc Reznicek, Anke Lüdeling, Cedric Krummes, and Franziska Schwantuschke. 2012. *Das Falko-Handbuch. Korpusaufbau und Annotationen Version 2.0*.

Alexandr Rosen, Jirka Hana, Barbora Štindlová, and Anna Feldman. 2013. Evaluating and automating the annotation of a learner corpus. *Language Resources and Evaluation*, pages 1–28.

Heike Telljohann, Erhard Hinrichs, and Sandra Kübler. 2004. The TüBa-D/Z treebank: Annotating German with a context-free backbone. In *Proceedings of the Fourth International Conference on Language Resources and Evaluation (LREC 2004)*, Lissabon.

Joel Tetreault and Martin Chodorow. 2008. Native judgments of non-native usage: Experiments in preposition error detection. In *Proceedings of the workshop on Human Judgments in Computational*

Linguistics at COLING-08, pages 24–32, Manchester, UK. Association for Computational Linguistics.

Weiyue Wang, Jan-Thorsten Peter, Hendrik Rosendahl, and Hermann Ney. 2016. CharacTer: Translation edit rate on character level. In *Proceedings of the First Conference on Machine Translation*, pages 505–510, Berlin, Germany. Association for Computational Linguistics.

Seid Muhie Yimam, Chris Biemann, Richard Eckart de Castilho, and Iryna Gurevych. 2014. Automatic annotation suggestions and custom annotation layers in WebAnno. In *Proceedings of 52nd Annual Meeting of the Association for Computational Linguistics: System Demonstrations*, pages 91–96, Baltimore, Maryland. Association for Computational Linguistics.

The Role of Diacritics in Adapting the Difficulty of Arabic Lexical Recognition Tests

Osama Hamed
Language Technology Lab
University of Duisburg-Essen
osama.hamed@uni-due.de

Torsten Zesch
Language Technology Lab
University of Duisburg-Essen
torsten.zesch@uni-due.de

Abstract

Lexical recognition tests are widely used to assess the vocabulary size of language learners. We investigate the role that diacritics play in adapting the difficulty of Arabic lexical recognition tests. For that purpose, we implement an NLP pipeline to reliably estimate the frequency of diacritized word forms. We then conduct a user study and compare Arabic lexical recognition tests in three settings: (i) without diacritics, (ii) with the most frequent diacritized form of a root, and (iii) the least frequent diacritized form of a root. We find that the use of infrequent diacritics can be used to adapt the difficulty of Arabic lexical recognition tests and to avoid ceiling effects.

1 Introduction

Lexical recognition tests (LRTs) are used to measure the vocabulary size of a learner. For that purpose, learners are presented with lexical items and have to decide whether they are part of the vocabulary of a given language (i.e. a *word*) or not (i.e. a *nonword*). Figure 1 gives an example of the two most common presentation formats: (i) Yes/No questions and (ii) checklists. A lexical recognition test consists of a relatively small number of words and nonwords, usually 40 words and 20 nonwords. It has been shown that such a small number of items is sufficient to consistently measure the vocabulary size (Huibregtse et al., 2002). As a consequence, lexical recognition tests are easy to administer and fast (Lemhöfer and Broersma, 2012).

Nonwords in a lexical recognition test are typically used as distractors. Thus, they should be close to existing words and are usually created by swapping letters in existing words (Stubbe, 2012) or by generating character sequences based

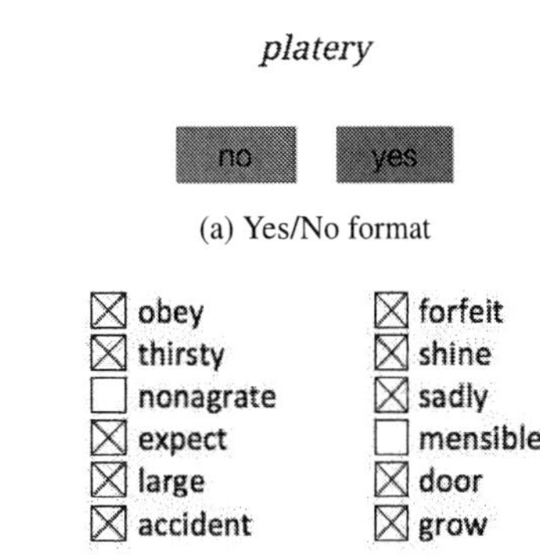

(a) Yes/No format

(b) Checklist format

Figure 1: Examples of lexical recognition tests.

on position-specific character language models (Hamed and Zesch, 2015). Words in a lexical recognition test have the function to measure the vocabulary size, thus the test needs to contain words from many frequency bands, i.e. very frequent words like *door* or *large* as well as less common words like *obey* or *forfeit*.

While lexical recognition tests are well-established for English (Lemhöfer and Broersma, 2012), and other European languages like German and Dutch (Lemhöfer and Broersma, 2012), French (Brysbaert, 2013) and Spanish (Izura et al., 2014), there is still very little work on Arabic LRTs. The studies by Baharudin et al. (2014) and Ricks (2015) neglect lexical diacritics, a very important feature of the Arabic language that causes many challenges for automatic processing (Farghaly and Shaalan, 2009).

The Arabic script contains two classes of symbols: letters and diacritics (Habash, 2010). Whereas letters are always written, diacritics are optional. Diacritics are usually used in specific settings like language teaching or religious texts. This leads to a high amount of ambiguity of a non-diacritized Arabic word. Figure 2 compares the

Osama Hamed and Torsten Zesch 2018. The role of diacritics in increasing the difficulty of Arabic lexical recognition tests. *Proceedings of the 7th Workshop on NLP for Computer Assisted Language Learning at SLTC 2018 (NLP4CALL 2018)*. Linköping Electronic Conference Proceedings 152: 23–31.

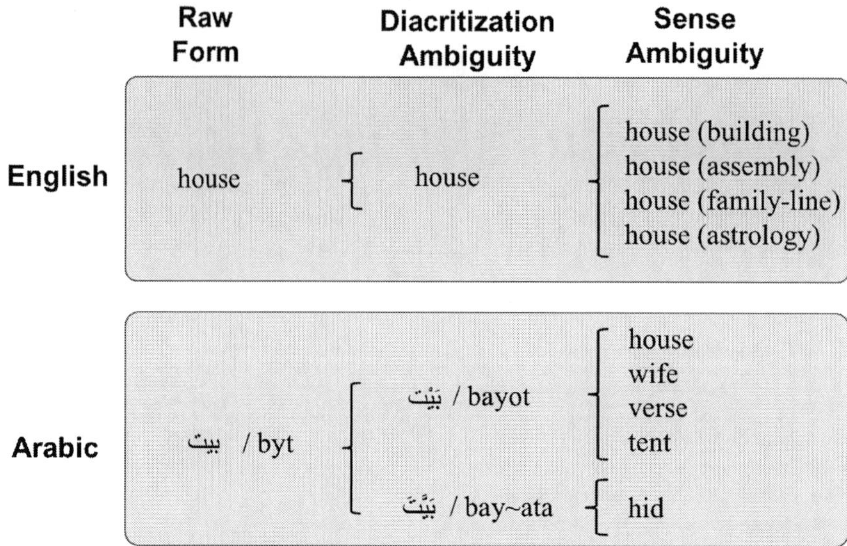

Figure 2: Sources of lexical ambiguity in English and Arabic (from (Hamed and Zesch, 2018)).

situation in English and Arabic. As English uses relatively few diacritics, there is no diacritization ambiguity. For example, the Arabic token بيت /byt/ has diacritizations like بَيْت /bayot/ and بَيَّتَ /bay~ata/. As can be seen in the last column in Figure 2, this issue is not to be confused with the sense ambiguity that exists in both English and Arabic on top of the diacritization ambiguity.

Recently, Hamed and Zesch (2017b) have shown that non-diacritized Arabic lexical recognition tests show serious ceiling effects as they are too easy for most learners. It is sufficient for a learner to recognize the root form as they know one of its diacritized forms – probably the most frequent diacritized of a word. Table 1 shows the frequency counts of some diacritized forms of the root /*kr/.[2]

Our hypothesis in this paper is that we can construct a more appropriate Arabic lexical recognition test by using less frequent diacritized forms,

Surface form	Diacritized form	Gloss	Counts
ذكر	ذَّكَر /*~akar/	Male	18
	ذِكْر /*ikor/	Prayer	10
	ذَكَرَ /*akar/	He mentioned	1454
	ذُكِرَ /*ukir/	It was mentioned	2001
	ذَّكَرَ /*~akar/	He reminded	1
	ذُكِّرَ /*uk~ir/	He was reminded	4

Table 1: Examples of diacritized forms of the Arabic word ذكر /*kr/.

such as /*ak~ara/ or /*uk~ira/. For that purpose, we first have to find a way to reliably estimate the frequency of diacritized word forms. Then, we conduct a user study, measuring the difficulty of the resulting lexical recognition test under three conditions: (i) No Diacritics: non-diacritized words, (ii) Frequent Diacritics: diacritized using the most frequent diacritized word form, and (iii) Infrequent-Diacritics: diacritized using the least frequent diacritized form of a word.

2 Counting Arabic Words

Obtaining reliable frequency counts for Arabic words is a task that entails a lot of NLP challenges regarding availability of corpora, automatic diacritization, segmentation, etc.

---

[2]The frequency counts are based on the Tashkeela corpus (Zerrouki and Balla, 2017), a corpus of classical Arabic books texts that are provided with diacritics.

Resource	Proportion
Aljazeera online	30%
Arabic Wikipedia	20%
Novels	15%
Alquds newspaper	10%
Altibbi	10%
IslamWeb	5%
Social networks (FB, Twitter)	5%
Other	5%

Table 2: Proportion of corpus resource.

2.1 Availability of Corpora

We typically need a large amount of diacritized Arabic text to estimate the frequency of diacritized word forms, but there is a lack of such resources. Generally, the currently available diacritized corpora are limited to Classical Arabic (usually religious text), such as the Holy Quran[3], Hadith books, RDI[4] and Tashkeela (Zerrouki and Balla, 2017); or Modern Standard Arabic (usually commercial news wires), such as Penn Arabic Treebanks (ATB) and Agence France Presse (AFP) that can be purchased from the Linguistic Data Consortium (LDC).

Source Corpus As the costs of acquiring annotated corpora can prevent researchers from conducting their research, we only want to use freely available corpora. One option is the provided by Zaghouani (2014) and contains newspaper articles crawled from the internet.[5]. However, as we are trying to build an educational application that measures language proficiency, we need text that covers a broader variety of topics. We are thus using the corpus introduced by Freihat et al. (2018), which was assembled from texts and text segments from a varied set of online Arabic language resources such as Wikipedia, news portals, online novels, social media, and medical consultancy web pages. Table 2 shows the distribution of sub corpora in the resource.

2.2 Automatic Diacritization

It has been shown that automatic diacritization can be used to obtain reliable frequency counts for Arabic words (Hamed and Zesch, 2018) by automatically diacritizing a large non-diacritized source corpus. According to a recent benchmark

(Hamed and Zesch, 2017a) comparing the available tools for diacritization (Farasa (Darwish and Mubarak, 2016), Madamira (Pasha et al., 2014) and two strong baselines), Farasa is outperforming the other approaches under all conditions. Therefore, we use Farasa to diacritize the crawled source corpus. The diacritized corpus is available upon request.

2.3 Lemmatization

As we want to use lemmas, not surface forms in our Arabic lexical recognition test, we need to perform lemmatization. This step is necessary as Arabic is a morphology-rich language and its words are highly inflected and derived (Aqel et al., 2015). Darwish and Mubarak (2016) reported that Farasa outperforms or matches state-of-the-art Arabic segmenters/lemmatizers like QCRI Advanced Tools For Arabic (QATARA) (Darwish et al., 2014) and Madamira (Pasha et al., 2014).

We (Hamed and Zesch, 2018) explore the effects of diacritization on Arabic frequency counts. We have shown that Farasa clearly gives better estimates than Madamira. Therefore, we integrate Farasa segmenter/lemmatizer in our NLP pipeline.

2.4 NLP Pipeline

To reliably estimate the frequency counts for the diacritized LRT word items, we run the following NLP pipeline, given the source corpus as input: (i) diacritize the source corpus using the Farasa diacritizer, (ii) segment the space-delimited diacritized words using Farasa, (iii) discard the extra clitics, (iv) label the roots with the corresponding diacritics with the help of DKPro Core[6], a collection of software components for natural language processing based on the Apache UIMA framework, and (v) assign the frequency counts for each root based on the attached diacritics.

After carrying out the aforementioned NLP pipeline on this source corpus, we will get frequency counts similar to that in Table 1. The frequency counts contain, among others, the most and least frequent diacritized form of a word that are corresponding to a given non-diacritized root/lemma. Now we are ready to construct the tests and conduct the user study.

---

[3]http://tanzil.net/download/

[4]http://www.rdi-eg.com/RDI/TrainingData/

[5]Available at: `https://sites.google.com/site/mouradabbas9/corpora`

[6]`https://dkpro.github.io/dkpro-core/`

Proceedings of the 7th Workshop on NLP for Computer Assisted Language Learning at SLTC 2018 (NLP4CALL 2018)

Word	Nonword	Swapped-letter
عاقل	عافل	ف to ق
بخ	بخ	خ to ح
معكوس	معكوش	ش to س

Table 3: Nonwords created by letter transposition

3 User Study Setup

In order to investigate the role of diacritical marks on improving the construct validity of Arabic lexical recognition tests, we conduct a user study where we compare three tests that differ in the diacritization settings.

- **No Diacritics (S1)**: We use the non-diacritized version of 'test A' as used by Hamed and Zesch (2017b). The nonwords have been generated using a letter substitution/transposition approach in an existing word. Table 3 contains some examples of such nonwords.

- **Frequent-Diacritics (S2)**: We diacritize all roots from S1 with the *most* frequent diacritized form. The nonwords are the same as in S1 and diacritized using a pronounceable (plausible) version of diacritics.

- **Infrequent-Diacritics (S3)**: We diacritize all words from S1 with the *least* frequent diacritized form. Figure 3 shows the resulting test in checklist format.

Pilot Study Before conducting the main user study, an Arabic teacher reviewed the three tests. For example, he made sure that no dialectal words are used because they could only be recognized by Arabic speakers of that dialect.

A few students (n = 11) were asked to participate in the user study, so that we check the overall format, design, and test instructions. No modifications have been made to overall test format or design. Minor modifications had to be made to test instructions after the pilot study.

Main Study First, we provide participants with a set of instructions including some sample items. Then the participants were asked to provide information about gender, age, mother tongue (L1), and the knowledge of Arabic language (number of

Figure 3: The diacritized tests items for test A in *infrequent-diacritics* setting (S3), words are checked, nonwords are not.

years they had taken Arabic courses). Then, participants had to finish the actual lexical recognition test. The test version which participants received (non diacritics, frequent diacritics, infrequent diacritics) was assigned randomly to avoid sequence effects.

Web Interface In order to conduct the study, we created a multi-device web interface using PHP and MySql database. Figure 4 shows how it looks like. We make the implementation available to allow for easy replication.[7]

---

[7] https://github.com/ohamed/ar-lrts

Figure 4: Web system.

	40 Words			**20 Nonwords**		
Test Setting	**P**	**R**	**F**	**P**	**R**	**F**
S1 – No Diacritics	.95	.95	.95	.93	.89	.91
S2 – Freq. Diac.	.91	.92	.91	.90	.82	.86
S3 – Infreq. Diac.	.92	.80	.86	.71	.85	.77

Table 4: Results for the three tests settings.

4 User Study Results

We advertised our study through different channels, such as mail listings and social media. Overall, 263 people participated in the study, 143 are male, 120 are female. The average age is 28.1 years. Overall, the participants are randomly distributed over the three tests as follows: 96 participants were assigned to S1, 78 participants were assigned to S2, and the remaining 89 participants were assigned to S3.

In Table 4, we show precision, recall, and F-measure for the three test settings for both words and nonwords, averaged over all participants. We see that while the precision for words is comparable over all three tests, our test version S3 with infrequent diacritics has lower recall. This is the intended effect or more people not recognizing the words (remember that the non-diacritized tests are too easy and we want people to fail a bit more often).

4.1 Comparing Test Versions

In order to compare the difficulty of the two diacritized tests S2 and S3 with the original non-diacritized test S1, we compute for each respondent a combined test score using the scoring scheme utilized by Hamed and Zesch (2017b). In order to account for the unequal number of words and nonwords in the test, it averages the corresponding recalls.

$$score(R) = \frac{(R_w + R_{nw}) \cdot 100}{2} \qquad (1)$$

This way, a yes bias – by identifying all items as words – (creating high error rates in the nonwords) would be *penalized* in the same way as a no bias – by identifying all items as nonwords – (causing high error rates for words), independently of the different numbers of words versus nonwords.

Then, we compute the average score (over all participants) for each variant. We obtain average scores of 91.8, 86.8, and 82.3 for the three tests respectively. We compute the statistical significance

of the differences between the three tests using the *t-test*. All differences between the scores are statistically significant.

We visualize the relationship between the setting and the scores obtained by the participants in each test as shown in Figure 5. The non-diacritized test S1 shows the predicted ceiling effect. The differences to the diacritized version with the most frequent diacritics (S2) are actually larger than we would have predicted (recall that our hypothesis was that even in the non-diacritized version, subjects would fall back to the most frequent diacritized form). However, in line with our predictions the third test version (S3) using infrequent diacritics is much more difficult than both other tests and shows no ceiling effects. It should thus be better suited for accurately measuring the vocabulary size of more advanced learners than the other test versions.

4.2 Item Analysis

So far, we have only looked at the test results in general (across all items), but it remains unclear whether all words get more difficult or whether the effect is stronger for some words.

Thus, we visualize the scores for each word in our three experimental settings using a heatmap along with their frequency counts as shown in Table 5. As the score corresponds to how many participants of our study recognized a word, light colors mean easy items and darker colors mean difficult items. We find that some words get much harder when using the least frequent diacritization, while there is almost no effect for other words. In order to check whether this effect can be attributed to the frequency of the underlying forms, we also plot the counts as obtained from the source corpus for the majority of the word items.[8]

Overall, there is no obvious relationship between the scores of the word in the three settings and their frequency counts. For example, هم /hm/ from S1 occurs 4,510 times, هُمْ /humo/ (meaning: *they*) from S2 occurs 2,388 times, and هَمّ /ham~/ (meaning: *worry*) from S3 occurs 57 times. How-

---

[8]The frequencies are obtained from the source corpus.

Arabic	Buckwalter Transliteration	S1 No Diac	S2 Freq. Diac	S3 Infreq. Diac	*freq* S1	S2	S3
عنصر	EnSr	.99	.91	.83	50	35	15
قتل	qtl	.98	.95	.95	416	184	77
قوة	qwp	.98	.92	.92	181	115	8
صعب	SEb	.98	.92	.84	132	41	1
أكثر	Okvr	.98	.95	.90	1561	1120	122
أساسي	OsAsy	.98	.95	.91	753	195	20
مدينة	mdynp	.98	.95	.84	98	80	2
يكفي	ykfy	.97	.94	.58	139	97	6
عكس	Eks	.97	.88	.90	101	99	2
نشر	n$r	.97	.90	.86	424	181	100
عدم	Edm	.97	.95	.91	931	640	133
طلب	Tlb	.97	.94	.89	399	192	7
خروج	xrwj	.97	.92	.68	481	158	21
فضل	fDl	.97	.92	.86	113	84	8
فكر	fkr	.97	.95	.85	332	305	12
قدرة	qdrp	.97	.95	.51	34	25	6
بيان	byAn	.97	.91	.91	883	370	3
يجعل	yjEl	.97	.94	.90	122	111	11
تحديد	tHdyd	.97	.94	.91	512	310	49
سلامة	slAmp	.96	.96	.66	34	26	6
عزيز	Ezyz	.96	.94	.92	472	304	42
علم	Elm	.96	.92	.92	348	279	4
صف	Sf	.96	.87	.70	131	38	9
وجه	wjh	.96	.92	.80	568	274	12
يتعلق	ytElq	.96	.90	.89	127	110	17
شبكة	$bkp	.96	.91	.81	22	19	1
محاولة	mHAwlp	.96	.94	.92	15	13	2
ذات	*At	.95	.87	.65	1234	205	42
إذ	I*	.95	.91	.31	328	302	11
مسؤولية	msWwlyp	.94	.94	.72	734	540	27
سلطة	slTp	.94	.91	.85	33	27	4
هم	hm	.94	.90	.93	4510	2388	57
إضافة	IDAfp	.94	.94	.91	325	197	5
مدة	mdp	.94	.95	.41	129	92	10
أخ	Ox	.93	.85	.25	38	33	5
يعني	yEny	.93	.91	.86	338	337	1
فنان	fnAn	.93	.87	.89	876	481	12
إحتلال	IHtlAl	.93	.90	.90	316	249	26
عانى	EAnY	.87	.87	.71	21	14	4
وحد	wHd	.65	.78	.86	335	326	5

Table 5: Heatmap visualizing the average score per word, along with their frequency counts. Items are sorted by S1 score.

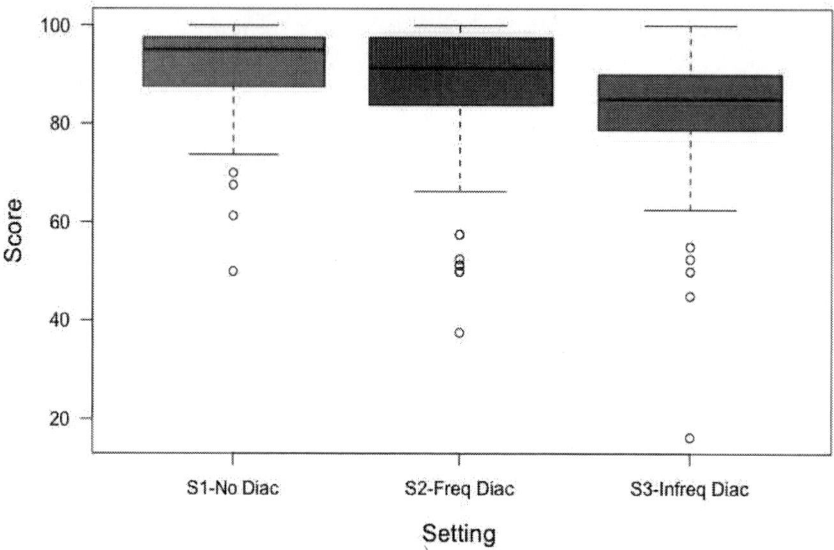

Figure 5: Visualization of the test scores under the three settings.

ever, we don't observe a big drop in the respective scores that are 94%, 93% and 90% for S1, S2, and S3.

5 Conclusion & Future Work

In this paper, we have shown that using Arabic lexical recognition tests with less frequent diacritized forms is a way to avoid the ceiling effects of previously proposed non-diacritized tests. We also show how the necessary frequency counts can be obtained by automatically diacritizing source corpora. In future work, we need to further investigate why some infrequent diacritized forms are hard while other (similarly infrequent) diacritized forms are easy. We hypothesize that the corpora used in this study might not reliably reflect the knowledge of learners. Also, even if we tried to minimize the effects of dialects, there might be strong influences from words being frequently used in a dialect or not.

Acknowledgments

We would like to thank *Andrea Horbach*, the Arabic teacher in the city of Duisburg *Mhamed ben Said*, and my colleagues from the *INDUS network*.

References

Afnan Aqel, Sahar Alwadei, and Mohammad Dahab. 2015. Building an Arabic Words Generator. *International Journal of Computer Applications*, 112(14).

Harun Baharudin, Zawawi Ismail, Adelina Asmawi, and Normala Baharuddin. 2014. TAV of Arabic language measurement. *Mediterranean Journal of Social Sciences*, 5(20):2402.

Marc Brysbaert. 2013. LEXTALE_FR: A fast, free, and efficient test to measure language proficiency in French. *Psychologica Belgica*, 53(1):23–37.

Kareem Darwish, Ahmed Abdelali, and Hamdy Mubarak. 2014. Using Stem-Templates to Improve Arabic POS and Gender/Number Tagging. In *LREC*, pages 2926–2931.

Kareem Darwish and Hamdy Mubarak. 2016. Farasa: A New Fast and Accurate Arabic Word Segmenter. In *Proceedings of the Tenth International Conference on Language Resources and Evaluation (LREC 2016)*, Paris, France. European Language Resources Association (ELRA).

Ali Farghaly and Khaled Shaalan. 2009. Arabic natural language processing: Challenges and solutions. *ACM Transactions on Asian Language Information Processing (TALIP)*, 8(4):14.

Abed Alhakim Ali Kayed Freihat, Gabor Bella, Mubarak Hamdy, Fausto Giunchiglia, et al. 2018. A single-model approach for arabic segmentation, pos-tagging and named entity recognition. In *International Conference on Natural Language and Speech Processing ICNLSP 2018*, Algiers, Algeria. ICNLSP.

Nizar Habash. 2010. Introduction to Arabic natural language processing. *Synthesis Lectures on Human Language Technologies*, 3(1):1–187.

Osama Hamed and Torsten Zesch. 2015. Generating Nonwords for Vocabulary Proficiency Testing. In *Proceeding of the 7th Language and Technology Conference: Human Language Technologies as a Challenge for Computer Science and Linguistics*, pages 473–477, Pozna, Poland.

Osama Hamed and Torsten Zesch. 2017a. A Survey and Comparative Study of Arabic Diacritization Tools. *JLCL: Special Issue - NLP for Perso-Arabic Alphabets.*, 32(1):27–47.

Osama Hamed and Torsten Zesch. 2017b. The Role of Diacritics in Designing Lexical Recognition Tests for Arabic. In *3rd International Conference on Arabic Computational Linguistics (ACLing 2017)*, Dubai, UAE. Elsevier.

Osama Hamed and Torsten Zesch. 2018. Exploring the Effects of Diacritization on Arabic Frequency Counts. In *Proceeding of the 2nd International Conference on Natural Language and Speech Processing (ICNLSP 2018)*, Algiers, Algeria.

Ineke Huibregtse, Wilfried Admiraal, and Paul Meara. 2002. Scores on a yes-no vocabulary test: Correction for guessing and response style. *Language testing*, 19(3):227–245.

Cristina Izura, Fernando Cuetos, and Marc Brysbaert. 2014. Lextale-Esp: A test to rapidly and efficiently assess the Spanish vocabulary size. *Psicológica*, 35(1):49–66.

Kristin Lemhöfer and Mirjam Broersma. 2012. Introducing LexTALE: A quick and valid lexical test for advanced learners of English. *Behavior Research Methods*, 44(2):325–343.

Arfath Pasha, Mohamed Al-Badrashiny, Mona Diab, Ahmed El Kholy, Ramy Eskander, Nizar Habash, Manoj Pooleery, Owen Rambow, and Ryan Roth. 2014. Madamira: A fast, comprehensive tool for morphological analysis and disambiguation of arabic. In *LREC*, pages 1094–1101.

Robert Ricks. 2015. The Development of Frequency-Based Assessments of Vocabulary Breadth and Depth for L2 Arabic.

Raymond Stubbe. 2012. Do pseudoword false alarm rates and overestimation rates in yes/no vocabulary tests change with japanese university students english ability levels? *Language Testing*, 29(4):471–488.

Wajdi Zaghouani. 2014. Critical survey of the freely available Arabic corpora. *In Proceedings of the International Conference on Language Resources and Evaluation (LREC'2014), OSACT Workshop. Rejkavik, Iceland.*

Taha Zerrouki and Amar Balla. 2017. Tashkeela: Novel corpus of Arabic vocalized texts, data for auto-diacritization systems. *Data in Brief*, 11:147–151.

An Automatic Error Tagger for German

Inga Kempfert and Christine Köhn
Natural Lanuguage Systems Group
Department of Informatics
Universität Hamburg
{5kempfer,ckoehn}@informatik.uni-hamburg.de

Abstract

Automatically classifying errors by language learners facilitates corpus analysis and tool development. We present a tag set and a rule-based classifier for automatically assigning error tags to edits in learner texts. In our manual evaluation, the tags assigned by the classifier are considered to be the best or close to best fitting tag by both raters in 91% of the cases.

1 Introduction

For a variety of tasks, it is useful to classify errors by language learners into error types. E. g. corpora which are annotated with error types can be used to extract examples for compiling teaching material or exercises. Errors can only be interpreted sensibly with respect to a reconstructed utterance, a so-called target hypothesis (TH) (Reznicek et al., 2013). An error type characterizes the divergence between the learner utterance and the corresponding TH.

Manually annotating error types is a time-consuming task and has to be repeated if an error tagging scheme changes. Therefore, automatic error tagging is desirable and in some use cases even inevitable when manual annotation is not feasible due to the amount of data (e. g. when selecting training data from Wikipedia edits for Grammatical Error Correction (GEC) systems (Boyd, 2018) or when evaluating the performance of GEC systems (Bryant et al., 2017)) or due to an interactive setting (automatic error tags could be used as an information source for student modeling and feedback generation if a reliable GEC system is available). In addition, automatic annotation has the advantage that it can be used to easily unify error annotations across different corpora as long as

	1	2	3		4	5		6
orig	Es	ist	**zeit**		für			Abendessen
TH2	Es	ist	**Zeit**		für	**das**		Abendessen
	It	*is*	*time*		*for*	*the*		*dinner*
tag			**S:ORTH**			**I:DET**		

Table 1: Example for two edits and their classification. The original text **orig** is aligned with the extended target hypothesis **TH2**. The edit at position 3 corrects a case error (error tag: **S:ORTH**), the other at position 5 inserts a determiner (**I:DET**). (ComiGS corpus, text 2mVs_2)

some form of correction is available[1].

Inspired by ERRANT (Bryant et al., 2017), a grammatical ERRor ANnotation Toolkit for extracting and classifying edits in English learner texts, we developed an error annotation tool for German: Gerrant. It classifies edits extracted from already aligned parallel learner corpora and assigns error tags using a rule-based approach. An example for two edits from the ComiGS corpus (Köhn and Köhn, 2018) and their error tags is shown in in Table 1.

We present the system, the error types and the design decisions that lead to this set. Although we have a rather large and diverse tag set, the assigned tags were regarded as best fitting in most of the cases in our manual evaluation.

2 Related Work

There have been several approaches to classifying edits in learner texts automatically in the past. The Falko corpus (Reznicek et al., 2012, 2013) which consists of essays written by learner of German was automatically annotated with simple tags

---

[1]The TH may be created automatically by a Grammatical Error Correction system. Grundkiewicz and Junczys-Dowmunt (2018) achieved a performance close to humans for English.

Inga Kempfert and Christine Köhn 2018. An automatic error tagger for German. *Proceedings of the 7th Workshop on NLP for Computer Assisted Language Learning at SLTC 2018 (NLP4CALL 2018)*. Linköping Electronic Conference Proceedings 152: 32–40.

Tag	Description
ADJ*	Adjective error
ADV*	Adverb error
CONJ*	Conjunction error
CONTR	Contraction error
DET*	Determiner error
MORPH	Morphological error
NOUN*	Noun error
OTHER*	Default category
ORTH	Orthography error
PREP*	Preposition error
PUNCT	Punctuation error
SPELL	Spelling error
VERB*	Verb error
WO	Word order error

Table 2: Main error categories. Every category can be prefixed with **S:** (substitution), categories marked with * can be combined with the prefixes **I:** (insertion) and **D:** (deletion). Word order errors have a special role (see text). Some categories have to be further specified to form a valid tag.

which classify the differences between the original and the target hypothesis based on the manual alignment into changes, insertions, deletions, merges, splits and movements.

ERRANT (Bryant et al., 2017) uses a more sophisticated approach and a broader tag set of 25 main error types for classifying edits in learner English. Most error types are based on the part of speech of the involved words. Since most of the types can be prefixed with ”M:” (Missing), ”R:” (Replacement) or ”U:” (Unnecessary edit), there are 55 error categories in total. ERRANT uses the ”linguistically-enhanced alignment algorithm” by Felice et al. (2016) for extracting the edits from a parallel corpus, which are then classified using a rule-based approach. ERRANT classifies edits based on automatically-obtained features such as PoS tag and dependency parse.

Recently, Boyd (2018) extended ERRANT to German and used it for enriching the training data for a GEC system by selecting edits from the German Wikipedia only for certain error types. This increased the performance of the GEC system over using all edits.

3 Error Types

Inspired by ERRANT and different manual error annotation schemes for German learner texts

(Rogers, 1984; Boyd, 2010), we developed our set of error categories and error tags. Every tag is prefixed by either **S:** (Substitution), **D:** (Deletion) or **I:** (Insertion). Table 2 lists the main error categories. Most categories are based on the PoS of the involved words. We call the combination of prefix and main error category a *coarse tag*. Nearly all PoS-based coarse tags have to be further specified to form a precise tag. This is done by appending subcategories to the coarse tag, e. g. the coarse tag **S:DET** can be extended to **S:DET:NUM** to form the precise tag for determiner error in number. The complete list of precise error tags is shown in Appendix A.

Insertions and deletions are either punctuation errors or certain PoS that have been inserted or deleted. Table 1 shows an example for inserting a determiner in the extended target hypothesis (TH2) from the ComiGS corpus (Köhn and Köhn, 2018).

Often an error involves more than one property of a word, e. g. a determiner might differ in case and gender. Therefore, we allow combinations of certain parts (see Appendix A) within the same coarse error tag with “_” (*and*), e. g. **S:DET:CASE_GEN** for determiner error in case and number. Some errors cannot be narrowed down to one error tag and we allow the combination of alternatives: Combinations are build with “:” between different error parts, e. g. **S:DET:CASE:GEN** means that the error is either a **S:DET:CASE** *or* a **S:DET:GEN** error, meaning Gerrant is unable to narrow down the error further[2]. Combinations of alternatives and conjunctions are also possible as in **S:DET:CASE_GEN:NUM** (a determiner error in case and gender or a determiner error in number).

Although the error tags are token-based, the verb error **S:VERB:SVA** (subject-verb agreement) includes syntactic errors but on the token level. Lexical confusions or semantic replacements are recognized either by the respective PoS-based category such as **S:VERB:-** if a verb was replaced with a semantically better fitting one or by **S:MORPH** if the tokens have the same stem, but different PoS.

If words are rearranged and changed at the same time, ERRANT classifies this only as a word order error or cannot recognize the word order error

---

[2]Note that even humans cannot always narrow the error down completely due to ambiguities

at all. In contrast, Gerrant treats word order errors as token-based, i. e. instead of rearranging a span of tokens, individual tokens are moved which allows for an additional error tagging of the moved tokens. Because of this, the tag for word order errors **S:WO** has a special role: It is an error tag on its own if the moved token was not changed but it can also be a prefix for another error type, e. g. if the word moved was change from lower to upper case this would be a tagged as **S:WO:ORTH**.

Currently, Gerrant does not automatically align the input texts and since it relies on a manual alignment being available, it has only been used on the Falko corpus and the ComiGS corpus. The detailed classification of word order errors only works on the ComiGS corpus because tokens in that corpus are aligned via a so-called tokmovid (tmid) if they have been moved (Köhn and Köhn, 2018).

Also contrary to ERRANT, Gerrant is able to assign an error tag to discontinuous word errors e. g. if the original text is *ist [...] liegend* ("is lying") and the TH *liegt* ("lies") and the tokens are annotated with a tokmovid, the error is tagged as **S:WO:VERB:FORM**, a combination of word order and verb form error. This is also important for classifying errors with separable verb prefixes because the verb and its prefix are often far apart (see **VERB:AVZ** in Table 5 in Appendix A).

4   Implementation and Rules

Gerrant uses several sources of information to classify an edit. It uses SpaCy[3] for dependency parsing, PoS tagging and lemmatization, Cistem[4] (Weissweiler and Fraser, 2018) for stemming and DEMorphy[5] (Altinok, 2018) for morphological analysis. We trained our own SpaCy model on the Hamburg Dependency Treebank (Foth et al., 2014) which uses the dependency scheme by Foth (2006) and the STTS tag set for PoS (Schiller et al., 1999).

Cistem is a state-of-the-art stemmer and segmenter for German and is available for several programming languages, including Python in which Gerrant is written. We chose Cistem over the Snowball stemmer provided by the python library nltk because it achieves better overall results.

We use DEMorphy's analyses for recognizing

morphological errors such as case or gender errors. DEMorphy is an off-the-shelf FST-based German morphological analyzer implemented in native Python. For reducing the set of possible analyses for one token, we use PoS tags of the original and the corrected tokens and the case information of the corrected tokens obtained from the dependency tree. The dependency tree is also used for identifying subject-verb agreement errors.

In Gerrant, an edit is checked for the different error types one after the other. First, the prefix is assigned, then the error type in accordance with the prefix. Insertion and deletion errors can only be classified as either a PoS error or a punctuation error. Edits with the prefix **S:** (Substitution) can be further classified by comparing not only the PoS but also morphological properties of the words on each side. Additionally, the edit has to be checked for spelling, orthographic, morphological and punctuation errors. Punctuation and orthographic errors are checked before PoS errors, spelling and morphological errors are checked for afterwards. The checks are all capsuled in different functions, which makes it easy to adjust the checks if need be.

For some error tags, it is sufficient to check if certain properties hold, e. g. for an orthography error **S:ORTH**, we only need to check whether case and/or whitespace is different between the words. For categories such as **DET**, there can be different readings for a word due to ambiguities: When processing a substitution error, we take all readings of the original token and all readings of the correction, try to narrow them down e. g. by case information from the dependency parse, and compare them pair-wise. For each pair, we combine all the differences with "_" (*and*) (e. g. **CASE_NUM**) and collect the differences for all pairs in one set. Then, we take the minimal subsets[6] of this set and combine them with ":" (*or*). This way, we end up with minimal diagnoses of the difference between the two tokens. The complete rule set can be found on Gerrant's website[7].

At this point, Gerrant only works on the ComiGS Corpus and the Falko corpus. The original text and the target hypotheses were already aligned in both corpora. In the Falko data, edits were already labeled with CHA (change), INS

---

[3]https://spacy.io/
[4]https://github.com/LeonieWeissweiler/CISTEM
[5]https://github.com/DuyguA/DEMorphy

[6]A minimal subset of a set S is a subset for which no other subset of S is also a subset.
[7]https://nats.gitlab.io/gerrant

	rater 1		rater 2		overall	
	coarse tag	precise tag	coarse tag	precise tag	coarse tag	precise tag
strongly agree	96.0	81.5	93.0	83.5	94.5	82.5
agree	0.5	11.0	1.5	9.5	1.0	10.25
disagree	0.0	1.0	1.0	1.5	0.5	1.25
strongly disagree	3.5	6.5	4.5	5.5	4.0	6.0

Table 3: Results of evaluation showing how much the human raters agree with the tags assigned by the system (in percent).

(insertion), DEL (deletion), MERGE, SPLIT and MOVS/MOVT (move source and move target). In the ComiGS corpus, the tokens are aligned and tokens which have been moved are labeled with a tokmovid.

For both corpora, we implemented individual readers converting them to the same edit format, which is passed to the error classifier. To make Gerrant accessible for other corpora, new readers can be added, that convert input data to an edit format that is processable by Gerrant. The edit format contains the original token, its absolute position in the text (optional), its position in the sentence, the error category, the corrected token, its absolute position in the text (optional), its position in the sentence and edit type.

5 Evaluation and Discussion

To evaluate Gerrant, we (the authors) manually rated the tags for 200 randomly chosen edits independently. One half was from the ComiGS corpus, the other from the FalkoEssayL2v2.4 corpus. For each of these sets, one half was from the minimal target hypothesis and one was from the extended target hypothesis.

The raters were given the original sentence, the corrected sentence, the edit and the tag assigned by the system. The raters were asked to judge on a 4-point Likert scale how appropriate the error tag is. Since there can be multiple tags for one coarse tag (combined with ":") and multiple parts combined in one tag (combined with "_") and we wanted to give partial credit for partially correct tags, the rating should be given as follows:

Strongly agree When the error in the text matches the error type in the description of the error tag exactly and no other tag fits better. If there are multiple tags combined with ":", every one of them fits exactly. Example 1: If **S:DET:NUM_CASE** is the best fitting tag and

Gerrant assigns exactly **S:DET:NUM_CASE**. Example 2: If Gerrant assigns **S:DET:CASE:GEN** and both **S:DET:CASE** and **S:DET:GEN** fit exactly.

Agree When Gerrant assigns one error type (without combinations of parts with ":") and the error matches the type but another error type fits better. Or: When Gerrant assigns a combination of error types (combinations of parts with ":") and the error matches one of the assigned error types in the description of the error tag, which include the best fitting label. Example: If **S:DET:NUM_CASE** is the best fitting tag and Gerrant assigns **S:DET:NUM_CASE:GEN**.

Disagree When the error matches the error type in the description of the error tag without the context. Considering the sentence context, the tag is incorrect. Or: If more than one tag was assigned, no label fits perfectly, but parts of the label are correct (e. g. if the assigned tag is **S:NOUN:CASE_NUM:-**, but it is only a **S:NOUN:NUM**).

Strongly disagree When the error does not match the error type described in the error tag description. If more than one error tag is assigned, not even partial tags fit.

If none of the above cases apply, the most appropriate rating should be chosen.

In addition to the precise error tags, the raters also evaluated the coarse error tags for the same edits. The coarse error tag consists of the prefix and the first part of the error tag, e. g. **S:NOUN** or **S:MORPH**. The coarse tag for all word order errors is **S:WO** even if the word error's precise tag classifies the error further as in **S:WO:NOUN:CASE**.

The evaluation results for both raters are shown in Table 3. When averaging over both annotators, Gerrant assigns the best or close to best fitting pre-

	1	2	3	4	5	6	7	8	9	10	11	12	13
orig	Er	**hat**	seinen	Mund	mit	die	Hand	**anzuhalten**	und	nur	gucken		
TH2	Er	**hält**	seinen	Mund	mit	der	Hand	zu	und		guckt	nur	**zu**
	He	*shuts-1*	*his*	*mouth*	*with*	*his*	*Hand*	*shuts-2*	*and*		*watches-1*	*only*	*watches-2*
tmid		1						1		2		2	

Table 4: Sentence which contains a complex verb error (positions 2 and 8, marked with tokmovid **tmid** 1) where two verb forms are jointly replaced by two other verb forms. (ComiGS Corpus, text 2mVs_1)

cise tag in 92.75% of the cases (coarse tag: 95.5%, see). While there is only a small difference between coarse and precise tags if "strongly agree" and "agree" are considered in sum, there is a considerable drop in "strongly agree" (−12 percentage points on average) and a considerable increase in "agree" (+9.25 percentage points on average). This shows that Gerrant most often assigns the best fitting coarse tag but not as often also the best fitting precise tag but only the close to best. In only 3% of the cases on average, the precise error tag was considered as not fitting (*disagree* or *strongly disagree*), although the coarse tag was considered fitting (*strongly agree* or *agree*).

Both raters give the same rating for the precise tags in 91.5% of the cases (coarse tag: 95.5%) and 91% of the precise tags are rated as *strongly agree* or *agree* by both annotators.

There are are a number of errors which Gerrant can improve on. Some error types do not behave as expected because Gerrant only extracts differences between the original and the correction, e. g. if the first word of a sentence is moved and the case is changed, this would be classified as an **S:WO:ORTH**, although technically it is not an orthographic error if the case was correct in the original text. For other error types, the rules can be further refined to match the tags more precisely: E. g. if the verb is changed by inserting the particle *zu* ("to") into the word as in *wegfahren* → *wegzufahren* ("to drive off"), Gerrant classifies this as a **S:VERB:AVZ**, although the separable verb prefix (*weg*) has not been changed. Currently insertions or deletions of the particle *zu* as a token on its own when it is not used as a separable verb prefix are classified as **OTHER**. It might be sensible to introduce an error category **PART** to cover all cases where the particle *zu* is deleted or inserted.

When a substitution error has more than one token on any side and the spans are not contiguous, Gerrant makes the simplifying assumption that this is always a word order error and uses **S:WO** as a prefix, although this might not be a word order error.

Gerrant can classify verb errors which contain more than one verb form on one side or both sides, e. g. for identifying tense errors. However, there are cases which Gerrant does not yet handle well: In the example in Table 5, the edit containing tokens 2 and 8 *hat anzuhalten* → *hält zu* ("has to stop" → "shuts") is tagged as a **S:WO:VERB:AVZ** error due to the differences in verb prefixes, although this should rather be modeled as a semantic and form error because *anzuhalten* ("to stop", an infinitive with the particle *zu*) was confused with *zuhalten* ("shut", a verb with the separable verb prefix *zu*).

Gerrant classifies verb errors based on the PoS of the original and the correction. Both sides must contain a verb form in order to check for verb errors. Because of this, some errors are not classified as verb errors due to the assigned PoS tags (an incorrect participle might be tagged as adjective and therefore is not treated as a verb).

Some improvements can also be made for recognizing **ADJ:FORM** and **ADV:FORM**, e. g. check if the adverb is accompanied with a particle (STTS tag: PTKA) or certain words such as *mehr* ("more").

Moreover, Gerrant could narrow down the assigned error tags further by taking more of the sentence context into account when disambiguating tokens.

6 Conclusions and Outlook

We presented Gerrant, an error annotation tool for German, which assigns error tags to given edits. Our evaluation shows that Gerrant chooses the most appropriate tag in the majority of cases. While the coarse tag is mostly correct, the precise tag is more often not the best fitting tag.

In future work, we plan to include more disambiguating information to further narrow down the possible error tags, currently the dependency tree is often used for disambiguating the corrected tokens but only rarely for the original tokens. Such information might also be useful for reducing the set of analyses of the original tokens.

In addition, word order errors are assigned in certain rare cases in the ComiGS corpus (due to a simplifying assumption) where no reordering has taken place. Also, word order errors are currently only treated token-based which allows for a straightforward further classification of the error. However, groups of moved or rearranged tokens should be combined into one error, which would require that error spans for different errors can overlap.

Until now Gerrant has only been used on manually aligned corpora. It should be extended to be able to automatically align input.

Gerrant can be downloaded from `https://nats.gitlab.io/gerrant`.

References

D. Altinok. 2018. DEMorphy, German Language Morphological Analyzer. *ArXiv e-prints*.

Adriane Boyd. 2010. EAGLE: an Error-Annotated Corpus of Beginning Learner German. In *Proceedings of the International Conference on Language Resources and Evaluation*, Valletta, Malta. European Language Resources Association (ELRA).

Adriane Boyd. 2018. Using Wikipedia Edits in Low Resource Grammatical Error Correction. In *Proceedings of the 4th Workshop on Noisy User-generated Text*.

Christopher Bryant, Mariano Felice, and Ted Briscoe. 2017. Automatic Annotation and Evaluation of Error Types for Grammatical Error Correction. In *Proceedings of the 55th Annual Meeting of the Association for Computational Linguistics (Volume 1: Long Papers)*, pages 793–805, Vancouver, Canada. Association for Computational Linguistics.

Mariano Felice, Christopher Bryant, and Ted Briscoe. 2016. Automatic Extraction of Learner Errors in ESL Sentences Using Linguistically Enhanced Alignments. In *Proceedings of COLING 2016, the 26th International Conference on Computational Linguistics: Technical Papers*, pages 825–835, Osaka, Japan. The COLING 2016 Organizing Committee.

Kilian A. Foth. 2006. *Eine umfassende Constraint-Dependenz-Grammatik des Deutschen*. Fachbereich Informatik, Universität Hamburg. URN: urn:nbn:de:gbv:18-228-7-2048.

Kilian A. Foth, Arne Köhn, Niels Beuck, and Wolfgang Menzel. 2014. Because size does matter: The Hamburg Dependency Treebank. In *Proceedings of the Language Resources and Evaluation Conference 2014*, Reykjavik, Iceland. LREC, European Language Resources Association (ELRA).

Roman Grundkiewicz and Marcin Junczys-Dowmunt. 2018. Near Human-Level Performance in Grammatical Error Correction with Hybrid Machine Translation. In *Proceedings of the 2018 Conference of the North American Chapter of the Association for Computational Linguistics: Human Language Technologies, Volume 2 (Short Papers)*, pages 284–290. Association for Computational Linguistics.

Christine Köhn and Arne Köhn. 2018. An Annotated Corpus of Picture Stories Retold by Language Learners. In *Proceedings of the Joint Workshop on Linguistic Annotation, Multiword Expressions and Constructions (LAW-MWE-CxG-2018)*, pages 121–132. Association for Computational Linguistics.

Marc Reznicek, Anke Lüdeling, and Hagen Hirschmann. 2013. Competing target hypotheses in the Falko corpus. In Ana Ballier Díaz-Negrillo and Paul Nicolas Thompson, editors, *Automatic Treatment and Analysis of Learner Corpus Data*, pages 101–123. John Benjamins Publishing Company, Amsterdam, NLD.

Marc Reznicek, Anke Lüdeling, Cedric Krummes, Franziska Schwantuschke, Maik Walter, Karin Schmidt, Hagen Hirschmann, and Torsten Andreas. 2012. *Das Falko-Handbuch*.

Margaret Rogers. 1984. On major types of written error in advanced students of German. *International Review of Applied Linguistics in Language Teaching*, 22(1):1–39.

Anne Schiller, Simone Teufel, Christine Stöckert, and Christine Thielen. 1999. Guidelines für das Tagging deutscher Textcorpora mit STTS. Technical report, Universität Stuttgart / Universität Tübingen.

Leonie Weissweiler and Alexander Fraser. 2018. Developing a Stemmer for German Based on a Comparative Analysis of Publicly Available Stemmers. In *Proceedings of the 27th International Conference of the German Society for Computational Linguistics and Language Technology (GSCL 2017): Language Technologies for the Challenges of the Digital Age*, pages 81–94, Cham. Springer International Publishing.

A Error Types

Categories which can be combined with **D:** (deletion) or **I:** (insertion) to form a precise error tag:

Category	Description
	insertion or deletion of
ADJ	adjective
ADV	adverb
CONJ:COORD	coordinating conjunction
CONJ:SUBORD	subordinating conjunction
DET	determiner
NOUN	noun
OTHER	(default category)
PREP	preposition
PRON	pronoun
PUNCT	punctuation
VERB	verb
VERB:AVZ	separable verb prefix

Category	Description	Example
ADJ:FORM	Either the token in the original sentence is not a valid form or the degree is incorrect.	*Der **freundlichere** Mann* → *Der **freundliche** Mann*
ADJ:INFL*	The inflection degree (weak/strong) of the adjective in the original text is incorrect	*Ein **schlafende** Löwe* → *Ein **schlafender** Löwe*
ADJ:NUM*	The number of the adjective in the original text is incorrect.	***Ungeduldiges** Pferde wiehern.* → ***Ungeduldige** Pferde wiehern.*
ADJ:CASE*	The case of the adjective in the original text is incorrect.	*Der **schlafendem** Löwe* → *Der **schlafende** Löwe*
ADJ:GEN*	The gender of the adjective in the original text is incorrect.	*Die **schöner** Frau geht spazieren.* → *Die **schöne** Frau geht spazieren.*
ADJ:-*	Any adjective error other than NUM, CASE, GEN, INFL and FORM e. g. the adjective was semantically replaced by a different one.	*Das **freundliche** Kind* → *Das **fröhliche** Kind*
DET:NUM*	The number of the determiner in the original text is incorrect.	***Das** Pferde stehen auf der Weide.* → ***Die** Pferde stehen auf der Weide.*
DET:CASE*	The case of the determiner in the original text is incorrect.	*Ich gebe **den** Hund den Ball.* → *Ich gebe **dem** Hund den Ball.*
DET:GEN*	The gender of the determiner in the original text is incorrect.	***Das** Hund bellt.* → ***Der** Hund bellt.*
DET:DEF*	The definiteness of the determiner in the original text is incorrect.	***Ein** Hund bellt.* → ***Der** Hund bellt.*
PRON:NUM*	The number of the pronoun in the original text is incorrect.	***Er** gingen nach Hause.* → ***Sie** gingen nach Hause.*
PRON:CASE*	The case of the pronoun in the original text is incorrect.	*Er gab mir **seiner** Jacke.* → *Er gab mir **seine** Jacke.*
PRON:GEN*	The gender of the pronoun in the original text is incorrect.	***Er** läuft.* → ***Sie** läuft.*

Category	Description	Example
PRON:-*	Any pronoun error other than NUM, CASE or GEN.	*Er rennt.* → **Wer rennt?**
NOUN:CASE*	The case of the noun in the original text is incorrect.	*Ich sehe das Auto des **Mann**.* → *Ich sehe das Auto des **Mannes**.*
NOUN:NUM*	The number of the noun in the original text is incorrect.	*Die **Ball** rollen.* → *Die **Bälle** rollen.*
NOUN:-*	Any noun error other than CASE or NUM e. g. the noun was semantically replaced by a differnt one.	*Das **Kalb** schlief.* → *Das **Fohlen** schlief.*
VERB:INFL	The verb is not a valid form.	*Die Vögel **fliegten**.* → *Die Vögel **flogen**.*
VERB:AVZ	The separable verb affix is incorrect in the original sentence	*Er **beibringt** seinem Sohn etwas.* → *Er **bringt** seinem Sohn etwas **bei**.*
VERB:FORM	The infinitive form is incorrect or the use of infinitive forms or participles is incorrect	*Das Kind **ist lesend**.* → *Das Kind **liest**.*
VERB:SVA*	Number and/or person of the verb in the original text are incorrect.	*Das Mädchen **spielen** draußen.* → *Das Mädchen **spielt** draußen.*
VERB:TENSE*	The tense of the verb in the original text is incorrect.	*Das Mädchen **spielt** draußen.* → *Das Mädchen **spielte** draußen.*
VERB:MODE*	Passive or subjunctive error in the original text.	*Das Mädchen **hätte** gespielt.* → *Das Mädchen **hat** gespielt.*
VERB:-*	Any verb error other than INFL, AVZ, FORM, SVA, TENSE or MODE	*Das Kind **hat gehend** nach Hause.* → *Das Kind **rannte** nach Hause.*
ADV:FORM	Either the token in the original sentence is not a valid adverb form or the degree of the adverb is incorrect.	*Ich tanze **guter** als du.* → *Ich tanze **besser** als du.*
ADV:-	Any adverb error e. g. the adverb was semantically replaced by a different one.	*Ich lese **immer**.* → *Ich lese **gerne**.*
CONJ:COORD	Both tokens are conjunctions for a coordinate clause.	*und* → *aber*
CONJ:SUBORD	Both tokens are conjunctions for a subordinate clause	*weil das Kind lief* → ***während** das Kind lief*
CONJ:-	Any conjunction error which is neither CONJ:COORD nor CONJ:SUBORD	*weil* → *aber*
CONTR	A preposition and a determiner were contracted to a preposition or a preposition was split into a preposition and a determiner.	*Ich gehe **zu das** Haus.* → *Ich gehe **zum** Haus.*
PREP	All involved tokens are prepositions.	*zu dem Tisch* → ***auf** dem Tisch*
PUNCT	Any punctuation error.	*.* → *,*
MORPH	Morphology error: The word in the original text and the target hypothesis have the same stem but have different PoS tags.	*Er **Liebe** sie* → *Er **liebt** sie*
OTHER	Default category if none of the error tags are applicable	
ORTH	Orthography error: Whitespace or case error	*hunde Korb* → *Hundekorb*

Category	Description	Example
SPELL	Spelling error where the original lemma is unknown and has a certain similarity to the corrected token.	*Weinahtcen* → *Weihnachten*
WO	Word order error	*Das Haus **blaue*** → *Das **blaue** Haus*

Table 5: Error categories which can be combined with the prefix **S:** to form a precise tag. * indicates that this tag can be combined with other tags in the same coarse category, e.g. case *or* number as in **S:ADJ:CASE:NUM** or case *and* number as in **S:ADJ:CASE_NUM**. Note that "-" cannot be combined with "_" (*and*). **WO** has a special role as it can be combined with any other category in this table (see Section 3).

Demonstrating the MUSTE Language Learning Environment

Herbert Lange and **Peter Ljunglöf**
Computer Science and Engineering
University of Gothenburg and Chalmers University of Technology

Abstract

We present a language learning application that relies on grammars to model the learning outcome. Based on this concept we can provide a powerful framework for language learning exercises with an intuitive user interface and a high reliability.

Currently the application aims to augment existing language classes and support students by improving the learner attitude and the general learning outcome. Extensions beyond that scope are promising and likely to be added in the future.

1 Introduction

In this paper we demonstrate MULLE, the MUSTE Language Learning Environment (Lange and Ljunglöf, 2018a). It is a versatile software system that doubles both as an authoring environment for language learning exercises and as a flexible language learning system.

It has an open architecture which makes it adaptable to many different use cases. The main use case we present here is in the context of a traditional language class based on a classic textbook. This limited context facilitates both conceptualization and development.

2 Features

The system we present employs many features to support a positive learning outcome.

The user interface is a system-independent web interface with low overhead that guarantees for intuitive user interactions by using a grammar-backed text editing method that works on the word level instead of on the character level (Ljunglöf, 2011). This method maps editing operations on the surface of a sentence onto modifications on the underlying syntax tree.

The learning process is structured following a schema of lessons and exercises. The whole language learning process is split into several lessons and each lesson consists of several exercises that have to be solved to pass a lesson. The lessons are based on multilingual translation grammars between a source language and the target language. Based on these lesson grammars a large set of exercises can be created, each exercise consisting of two sentences, and the learner's task is to use the above-mentioned text editing method to change one of the sentences to make it a proper translation of the other.

The reliance on grammars for modeling the lesson structure as the foundation for the learning process places the approach close to Controlled Natural Languages (Kuhn, 2014) that are well-known for a high reliability for example for transfer-based machine translation. Instead of using the grammars for translation we use them to generate translation exercises but we can provide the same level of reliability (Lange and Ljunglöf, 2018b).

The type of exercises that are generated by our system can be seen as related to Cloze or fill-in-the-blank tests (Taylor, 1953; O'Toole and King, 2011), but much more general. Instead of using corpora to create exercises, we rely on grammars, an idea that also has been explored by (Perez-Beltrachini et al., 2012).

To support the learner motivation we include aspects of gamification. Based on ideas from the Gameflow framework (Sweetser and Wyeth, 2005) we provide *Concentration*, i.e., minimizing the distraction from the task,

Herbert Lange and Peter Ljunglöf 2018. Demonstrating the MUSTE language learning environment. *Proceedings of the 7th Workshop on NLP for Computer Assisted Language Learning at SLTC 2018 (NLP4CALL 2018)*. Linköping Electronic Conference Proceedings 152: 41–46.

Challenge by giving a scoring schema, *Control* by providing an intuitive way to modify the sentence, *Clear goals* by providing a lesson structure, and *Immediate feedback* with a color schema to highlight the translation progress.

3 Learner Interaction

Each exercise consists of two sentences in different languages, one language that the user already knows (the *metalanguage*), and the language to be learned (the *object language*). Both sentences differ in some respect, depending on the grammatical features that the lesson is focusing on.

The user interacts with the system by incrementally modifying the object language sentence until it is a correct translation of the metalanguage sentence. The edit operation is based on the work of Ljunglöf (2011).

The editing interaction is done on the word-level, which means that the user is not allowed to enter arbitrary words, phrases or sentences from the keyboard. There are several reasons for this, but one reason is to avoid problems with unknown words and phrases, which is a risk with systems that are supposed to handle free text input (Heift, 2001, section 3). Another reason for disallowing free text input is to make the system accessible for alternative input methods such as mobile phone touch screens.

There are two possible editing operations:

- The user can select (i.e., click, point or otherwise specify) a word (or a phrase) in the text. The system interprets this as a request to either delete the word/phrase, or to replace it with another word (or phrase).

- Alternatively the user can select the space between two words, which is interpreted as a request to insert a new word or phrase.

When the user performs an editing operation, the system searches for similar sentences according to the grammar, and presents them in a menu. The user can select one of the suggestions, or they can reject the suggestions by selecting something else.

The suggestions that are presented are always grammatically correct according to the lesson grammar. This is done by parsing the original sentence, then modifying the syntax trees while keeping them correct according to the grammar, and then linearising the modified trees.

The system tries to be intelligent in the way that it knows which tree nodes are modified, and since it knows which surface words these nodes are responsible for, it can designate each modified sentence to a specific selection of the surface sentence.

3.1 An Illustrative Example

In this example we assume that the metalanguage is English (meaning that the user already knows English), and the object language is Latin (i.e., the language that the user is learning). All screenshots are found as figures 2–5, in appendix A.

The exercise consists of translating the English sentence *"many kings love Paris"* into Latin. As a starting point we have the Latin sentence *"rex librum legit"*, meaning *"a king reads a book"* (or *"the king reads the book"*, since Latin doesn't make a difference between definite and indefinite form).

Figure 2 shows how the exercise screen looks at the start. Note that the words that already match each other (*"king"* vs *"rex"*) are highlighted in green.

Now we have to select something in the Latin sentence to modify. We start with selecting the verb *"legit"* (eng. *read*), and the system shows a menu of possible verbs to replace with. We select the correct verb *"amat"* (eng. *love*), and the Latin sentence changes. Now two words are highlighted because they are matching with the English sentence. (See figure 3).

Second we decide to insert a determiner corresponding to the English word *"many"*. We click in front of the first word and the system displays a menu with different determiners. After selecting the word *"multi"*, the sentence changes, and there are three highlighted words. (See figure 4).

Note that the inflection form of *rex* changes to *reges*, because the number of the determiner changed from singular to plural. Also note that *amat* changes to *amant* for exactly the same reason.

Proceedings of the 7th Workshop on NLP for Computer Assisted Language Learning at SLTC 2018 (NLP4CALL 2018)

Finally, we change the noun *"librum"* (eng. *book*) into the proper name *"Lutetiam"* (*Paris*), and the exercise is solved. (See figure 5).

4 Under The Hood

In this section we give a very brief explanation of how the system works under the hood.

A lesson is defined by a grammar that is bilingual, in the sense that both languages share a common syntactic representation. This language-independent syntax is called *abstract syntax*, and for each language there is a mapping from the abstract syntax to the *concrete syntax* for that language. This mapping is called *linearisation*, and its inverse is called *parsing*.

Since languages are inherently ambiguous, several different syntax trees can linearise to the same string. Therefore, we represent each sentence as the set of all its parse trees. The goal of an exercise is to make the object language sentence a translation of the meta-language sentence, and the system tests that by checking if the first sentence has at least one parse tree in common with the second sentence.

4.1 Populating The Menus

Text editing in this system consists of the user selecting modifications of the sentence from one of its menus. The menus are populated like this:

1. First we collect the linearisations for syntax trees that are similar to some parse tree of the original sentence.

2. For each modified linearisation, we decide which words are changed from the original sentence. The affected words (or spaces between words) in the original sentence are called the *selection*.

3. Every selection has a corresponding menu, to which we add the modified linearisation.

The main problem in this procedure is how to find similar syntax trees. We use an idea similar to adjunction in TAG, Tree Adjoining Grammar (Joshi and Schabes, 1997), where we "cut out" a clique of nodes from the tree and replace them with another clique so that the new tree is still grammatical. These connected nodes that we cut out are similar to the auxiliary trees in TAG, as are the ones we put back into the tree. To reduce the number of menu items, we also filter out all similar trees that can be reached in two smaller steps.

4.2 The Grammar Formalism

The grammar formalism that we use in our implementation is Grammatical Framework (Ranta, 2011), because it has very good support for multilingualism, abstract and concrete syntax, and an extensive Resource Grammar Library for up to 30 languages (Ranta, 2009).

Note that all algorithms, and the implementation of the system as a whole, are independent of the grammars and the meta- and object languages. This means that the only thing we have to do to make the system work between e.g. Swedish and French, is to change the bilingual grammar.

5 Lesson Authoring

Traditionally, a language class relies on a textbook which provides the learner with a sequence of lessons, each consisting of a text fragment, a vocabulary list and some exercises to be solved on paper. This approach tends to be inflexible and unappealing to students, especially concerning translation exercises. We remedy this drawback by providing flexibility to this kind of exercise and use a game-like computer system to present them to the learner.

To be able to do this we have to transform the information available in the textbook into a set of lesson grammars. The process of creating a lesson grammar from a textbook lesson consists of three steps. These steps should be automated as much as possible, but at the moment require some human intervention. The steps are the following:

(a) Adapt a lexicon from the textbook lesson, which usually is given as an explicit vocabulary list. Available lexical and morphological resources can be reused.

(b) Create syntax trees for all sentences in the text. This can be done manually

Augustus   (m)   name of an emperor
Caesar   (m)   name of an emperor
                        (later used as title)
imperator, -oris (m)   emperor
Romanus, -a, -um   Roman
est   (he/she/it) is

```
PN  ::=  "Augustus"
N   ::=  "Caesar"  |  "imperator"
A   ::=  "Romanus"
V   ::=  "est"
```

(a) Formalize the vocabulary from the textbook (top) as a Grammar lexicon (bottom)

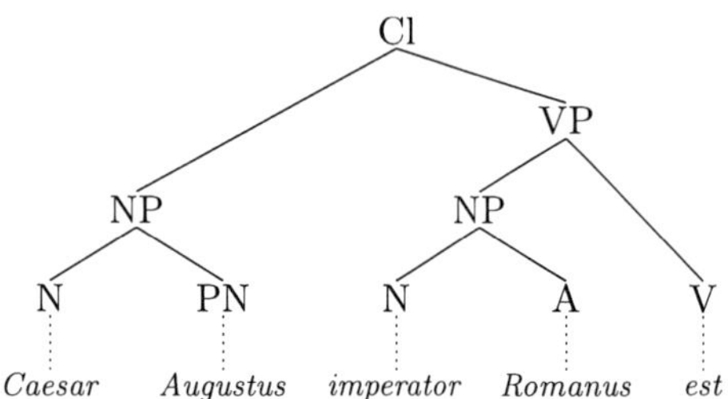

(b) Create a syntax tree to cover the sentence

```
NP  ::=  N PN  |  A N
VP  ::=  V NP
Cl  ::=  NP VP
S   ::=  Cl
```

(c) Derive a grammar from the syntax trees

Figure 1: The steps to derive a grammar from a sentence

or semi-automatically by parsing the sentences with an extensive grammar like the ones available in the Resource Grammar Library extended with the new lexicon. In case of several analyses, the correct, i.e. desired, analysis has to be selected manually.

(c) Create a new grammar describing precisely the trees from the previous steps. For that the rules can be read off the inner nodes of the trees. Usually this grammar will be over-generating. Several methods can be used to reduce the grammar, e.g. by merging several rules to one. These grammars can be implemented by using a subset of a Resource Grammar from the Resource Grammar Library.

An example of this process can be seen in Figure 1. The last two steps can profit from having access to the Resource Grammar Library. It makes it easy to add additional languages to a lesson or exchange one language for another, thanks to a high level of abstraction.

The grammar which we get as a result from this process can be used in our application to generate translation exercises based on the content of a syllabus and in the context of a language course. In the end each lesson is covered by one grammar which is specific to exactly the same vocabulary and syntactic complexity of this lesson. This means that the content of the exercises generated from this lesson grammar should already be familiar to a student from the classroom.

To create exercises within a lesson, pairs of sentences have to be selected. These sentences have to be covered by the lesson grammar and it should be within the current abilities of the learner to transform one of the sentences in a way that makes it a proper translation of the other one.

So in conclusion we can say, that a lesson in MULLE consists both of a multilingual grammar including both the meta- and the object language and a set of exercises, i.e. pairs of sentences covered by this grammar. To finish a lesson a subset of these exercises have to be solved.

6   Discussion

The current focus is on supporting existing language classes in a closed classroom setting. This focus is not new and has already some history within the use of machine translation technology for language learning (Richmond, 1994). This is for most languages still the most common way to teach and learn them. However, depending on the language and the context, different kinds of language competence can be the goal of the language classes. Sometimes just translation competence is required while in other circumstances extensive communicative competence is the ultimate goal.

Especially historic languages belong to the first category while most of the modern languages belong to the second. The framework we present here has relevant properties that make it especially suitable for historic languages but it can also be adapted to support language learners that aim for more than just translation competence.

The relevant properties for historic languages are:

- Tackling data sparseness with a grammar-based approach

- Combination of traditional and modern methods of teaching to improve learner motivation

- Both flexible and reliable exercises with high level of control over content

For modern languages additional exercises can be added for the future. These exercises can include among others:

- Morphology exercises to train word forms and agreement

- Graphical exercises containing image description tasks

- Listening exercises

The first kind of exercises can be created by temporarily relaxing grammatical constraints which can be done automatically given grammars in a suitable formalism like Grammatical Framework. The other two exercise types are possible because a sufficiently expressive grammar formalism can not only describe string languages, but can as well express procedures for picture generation or search terms for audio samples in a uniform way.

A pilot evaluation already showed interest in this kind of application both among teachers and students which leads to a concrete plan for the near future. This includes first a full evaluation followed by the extensions sketched here.

References

Trude Heift. 2001. Intelligent Language Tutoring Systems for Grammar Practice. *Zeitschrift für Interkulturellen Fremdsprachenunterricht*, 6(2).

Aravind K. Joshi and Yves Schabes. 1997. Tree-adjoining grammars. In Grzegorz Rozenberg and Arto Salomaa, editors, *Handbook of Formal Languages. Vol 3: Beyond Words*, chapter 2, pages 69–123. Springer-Verlag.

Tobias Kuhn. 2014. A Survey and Classification of Controlled Natural Languages. *Computational Linguistics*, 40(1):121–170.

Herbert Lange and Peter Ljunglöf. 2018a. MULLE: A Grammar-based Latin Language Learning Tool to Supplement the Classroom Setting. In *Proceedings of the 5th Workshop on Natural Language Processing Techniques for Educational Applications (NLPTEA '18)*, pages 108–112, Melbourn. Australia. Association for Computational Linguistics.

Herbert Lange and Peter Ljunglöf. 2018b. Putting Control into Language Learning. In *SIGCNL 2018*, Maynooth, Ireland.

Peter Ljunglöf. 2011. Editing Syntax Trees on the Surface. In *Nodalida'11: 18th Nordic Conference of Computational Linguistics*, Rīga, Latvia.

J.M. O'Toole and R.A.R. King. 2011. The deceptive mean: Conceptual scoring of cloze entries differentially advantages more able readers. *Language Testing*, 28(1):127–144.

Laura Perez-Beltrachini, Claire Gardent, and German Kruszewski. 2012. Generating grammar exercises. In *Proceedings of the Seventh Workshop on Building Educational Applications Using NLP*, NAACL HLT '12, pages 147–156, Stroudsburg, PA, USA. Association for Computational Linguistics.

Aarne Ranta. 2009. The GF Resource Grammar Library. *Linguistic Issues in Language Technology*, 2(2).

Aarne Ranta. 2011. *Grammatical Framework: Programming with Multilingual Grammars*. CSLI Publications, Stanford.

Ian M. Richmond. 1994. Doing It Backwards: Using Translation Software To Teach Target-Language Grammaticality. *Computer Assisted Language Learning*, 7(1):65–78.

Penelope Sweetser and Peta Wyeth. 2005. Game-Flow: A Model for Evaluating Player Enjoyment in Games. *Computers in Entertainment (CIE)*, 3(3):3–3.

Wilson L. Taylor. 1953. "cloze procedure": A new tool for measuring readability. *Journalism Quarterly*, 30(4):415–433.

A Screenshots From An Exercise Session

See section 3.1 for a deeper explanation of the screenshots in this appendix.

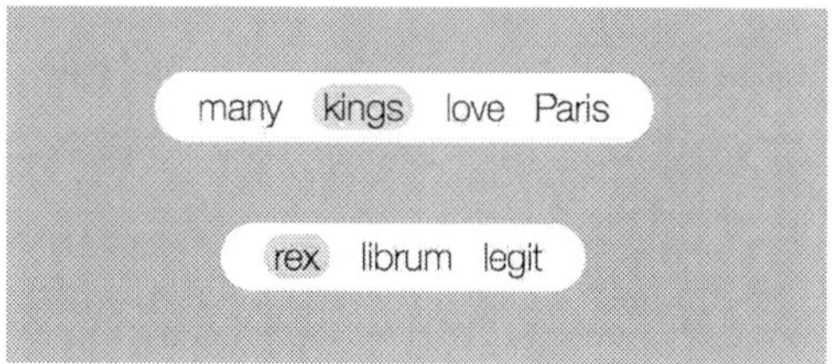

Figure 2: Beginning of the exercise – the lower Latin sentence means *a king reads a book*

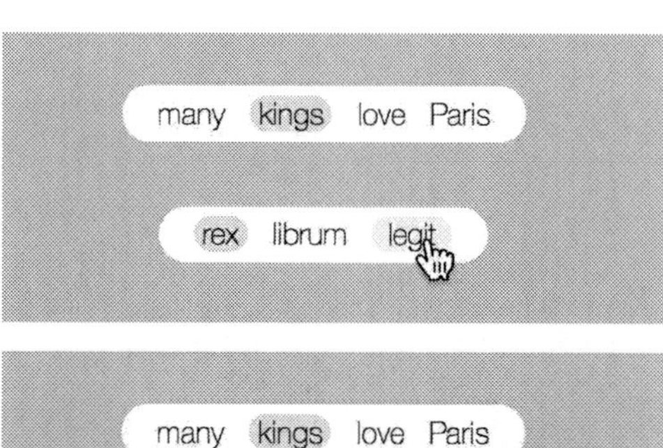

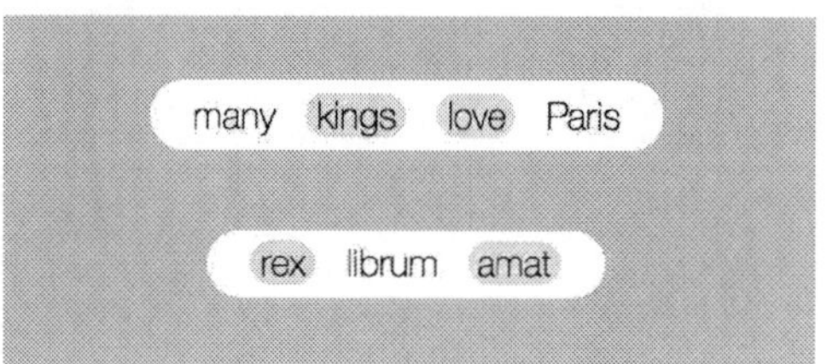

Figure 3: Replacing the verb *legit* (eng. *read*) with *amat* (eng. *love*)

Figure 4: Inserting the determiner *multi* (eng. *many*) before *rex* (eng. *king*)

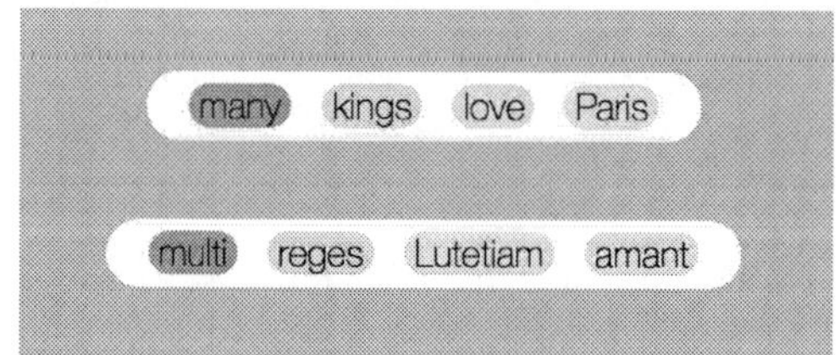

Figure 5: Replacing the noun *librum* (eng. *book*) with *Lutetiam* (eng. *Paris*)

Learner Corpus Anonymization in the Age of GDPR:
Insights from the Creation of a Learner Corpus of Swedish

Beáta Megyesi[1], Lena Granstedt[2], Sofia Johansson[3], Julia Prentice[4], Dan Rosén[4], Carl-Johan Schenström[4], Gunlög Sundberg[3], Mats Wirén[3] & Elena Volodina[4]

[1]Uppsala University, [2]Umeå University, [3]Stockholm University, [4]University of Gothenburg, Sweden

swell@svenska.gu.se

Abstract

This paper reports on the status of learner corpus anonymization for the ongoing research infrastructure project SweLL. The main project aim is to deliver and make available for research a well-annotated corpus of essays written by second language (L2) learners of Swedish. As the practice shows, annotation of learner texts is a sensitive process demanding a lot of compromises between ethical and legal demands on the one hand, and research and technical demands, on the other. Below, is a concise description of the current status of pseudonymization of language learner data to ensure anonymity of the learners, with numerous examples of the above-mentioned compromises.

1 Introduction

SweLL—Swedish Learner Language—is a project aimed at setting up an electronic infrastructure for collecting, annotating, searching and analyzing Swedish learner language (Volodina et al., 2016a). During the first year of the project, a number of the project aims related to the questions of data accessibility for the research community have been addressed, such as

1. legal and ethical aspects of essay collection,

2. principles of learner language anonymization and pseudonymization, and

3. tools and platforms for ensuring the previous steps.

Annotation in general is where linguistics – as well as pedagogy and other disciplines – nowadays hide in Natural Language Processing (NLP) (Fort, 2016). (Annotated) L2 data is extensively used for research, for instance within NLP, Second Language Acquisition (SLA) and Learner Corpus Research (LCR), and thus the annotation should be reliable, reproducible, and comparable between different corpora, so that conclusions drawn from the data are also reliable. But above all the data needs to be open outside the original project where it has been collected, a challenge that is not so easy to address with the new European Union (EU) General Data Protection Regulation (GDPR)[2]. The demands that we face require careful analysis of what makes the data sensitive and we need to take all possible precautions to reduce the risks of illegal or unethical use of the data before it can be made accessible.

To ensure that the data collected in the project can be used openly in research, we have worked extensively on legal issues, data handling flow, anonymization principles and tools in support of anonymization. Below, we describe the first steps and insights taken in SweLL.

1.1 SweLL infrastructure

The purpose of the SweLL project is to set up an infrastructure for continuous collection, digitization, normalization, and annotation of texts written by learners of Swedish as a second language. The aim is to make available (as open access) a linguistically annotated corpus consisting of a collection of approx. 600 learner texts and tools for automatic processing of these texts by allowing search and download for registered users (Volodina et al., 2016a).

The texts in the collection are produced by learners of Swedish as a second language from the age of 16 on voluntary basis given their consent. The texts are collected in schools where education is given in Swedish as a Second Language such as Swedish for Immigrants (SFI) or Swedish as

https://spraakbanken.gu.se/eng/swell_infra

[2]https://gdpr-info.eu

Beáta Megyesi, Lena Granstedt, Sofia Johansson, Julia Prentice, Dan Rosén, Carl-Johan Schenström, Gunlög Sundberg, Mats Wirén and Elena Volodina 2018. Learner corpus anonymization in the age of GDPR: Insights from the creation of a learner corpus of Swedish. *Proceedings of the 7th Workshop on NLP for Computer Assisted Language Learning at SLTC 2018 (NLP4CALL 2018)*. Linköping Electronic Conference Proceedings 152: 47–56.

second language, or where learners are tested for their proficiency in Swedish, such as CEFR (Common European Framework of Reference (Council of Europe, 2001)) or TISUS (Test In Swedish for University Studies (Volodina et al., 2016b)). Our aim is, by the end of the project, to have collected and annotated at least 600 texts and exercise answers written in response to tasks given by the teachers to students in schools, along with additional metadata information about the learners and the writing task.

We envisage a multi-purpose environment that combines data collection, algorithms for automatic processing of data, visualization analytic tools and L2 task generation. SweLL creates an infrastructure consisting of:
1. a data collection portal, through file import and via online exercises,
2. an annotated corpus of written L2 production,
3. methods and tools for L2 analysis, and
4. specific search tools for L2-material facilitating filtering for e.g. writers of a certain mother tongue, or writers at a certain proficiency level.

The material and tools will be made accessible through the learning platform Lärka (Volodina et al., 2014) created and maintained by Språkbanken at Gothenburg University. Lärka has up to now been a login-free online tool used for teaching Swedish grammar to university students and for deploying prototype exercises for learners on Swedish vocabulary. Lärka is extended to include a portal for collecting and processing L2 corpora, and linked to Korp (Ahlberg et al., 2013) and Strix - two tools under development at Språkbanken - for browsing texts and visualization of statistics and analytics.

In the long term, the data in terms of the collected essays and information about the learner, along with its reliability—and above all its accessibility—are the most important issues in the SweLL electronic infrastructure. To assure long-term usage and open access to the SweLL data collection, we were keen to adhere to current law and regulations in the SweLL data management flow.

2 Legal issues and learner corpora

2.1 Data protection and free access

The European Union's new General Data Protection Regulation (Regulation EU 2016/6791), enforced on May 25 2018, regulates the processing of personal data related to individuals by an individual, a company or an organization in the EU. Personal data "means any information relating to an identified or identifiable natural person ('data subject'); an identifiable natural person is one who can be identified, directly or indirectly, in particular by reference to an identifier such as a name, an identification number, location data, an online identifier or to one or more factors specific to the physical, physiological, genetic, mental, economic, cultural or social identity of that natural person" (Article 4, EU GDPR).

GDPR demands that stored data containing personal information undergo either an anonymization or a pseudonymization process. *Anonymization* is the removal of all personal identification so that the person is not or no longer identifiable. Thus, the data must be stripped of any identifiable information, making it impossible to derive insights on a certain individual, even by the party that is responsible for the anonymization. Anonymous data cannot be re-identified. *Pseudonymization* according EU GDPR (Article 4) is "the processing of personal data in such a manner that the personal data can no longer be attributed to a specific data subject without the use of additional information, provided that such additional information is kept separately". "Additional information" is typically a translation table by which pseudonymized personal data can be mapped back to the original data. But since this "additional information" should be the *only* means to re-identify a person, a consequence is that it must not be possible to do re-identification with the help of *other* information openly available, for example, on the Internet or in public registers, or by coordinated processing of such information[3]. This is what put such high demands on pseudonymization.

Contemporary trends in modern research has caused an increase in building large infrastructures in support of research. With respect to data collection, an electronic research infrastructure ideally consists of: (Volodina et al., 2016a):

1. freely accessible data in electronic format,
2. a technical platform for exploring the data, including tools and algorithms for data analysis, and visualization,
3. a set of tools and technical solutions for new data collection and preparation, including data processing and annotation, and

---

[3]in Swedish: "samkörning"

4. relevant expertise within the area.

On the one hand, the most important aspect for research as promoted by the major granting offices is *freely accessible data* in electronic format. On the other hand, modern legislation makes it more and more difficult to collect data for open use in research, especially in connection to the recently adopted GDPR, which sets to protect *data subjects' integrity*, and which—in combination with Swedish legislation on open access to public data (Riksdagen, 1949, ch.2)—sets certain limitations on the metadata types we are able to collect and types of information that we are able to keep in the original texts, see discussion of that in Volodina et al. (2018).

2.2 Pseudonymization in learner corpora

Out of the above follows the need to take precautions not only when it concerns the metadata, but also when it comes to the contents in the learner-written texts. This step usually takes form of pseudonymization—a general term which covers all possible ways of manipulating such information in the texts that can reveal an author behind them. This information might include, for example, person name, age, locations like home town, address, work place, family related issues, or text items revealing information that can be used for any kind of discrimination, being it political views, religious convictions, or sexual orientation.

To minimize the chance that personal data records and identifiers lead to the identification of subjects, all identifiers in the essays need to be overseen, masked and eventually replaced to ensure anonymity. Thus, pseudonymization includes the identification of personal information that can relate to the subject (e.g. My name is *Ali*), and the classification of that information, masked into certain predefined types (e.g. My name is *first_name*). Each information type can then be replaced in a systematic way to reproduce a "natural" text to increase reading flow (e.g. My name is *Robert* where the original first name is replaced randomly by another first name).

There are several ways to mask the sensitive information in the pseudonymization process, among others through substitution (e.g. Poland →Greece); by making text noisy (e.g. Poland →Europe); or by completely removing a text segment.

Different approaches to pseudonymization (which is also often called anonymization in the NLP literature, see e.g. Medlock (2016)) are used across learner corpus projects[4]. For instance, in CzeSL (Rosen, 2017) all names are substituted with *Adam*, *Eva* or *Sin*, in corresponding morphologically inflected forms, preserving possible spelling errors in suffixes or endings. In many other cases the notation uses codes, e.g. village<priv>. In ASK (Tenfjord et al., 2006), codes in the format @*name*, @*place*, @*something*, etc. replace the original tokens (Tenfjord et al., 2006). In CroLTec (Preradović et al., 2015), replacement of names was hard-coded during the error annotation without any special guidelines. Essays containing political views and other sensitive information were discarded from the corpus. Next, we will describe the SweLL approach to protect the anonymity of the learners.

3 Data management and pseudonymization in SweLL

In order to assure that the collection and access of the texts written by the learners (i.e. the subjects) comply with applicable laws and regulations, especially GDPR, the data needs to be handled in a secure way during collection and storage, and the subjects in the corpus must be de-identified. *De-identification* occurs when data has been stripped of common identifiers such as names, age, geographic places, dates, telephone numbers, e-mail addresses, personal web-URLs, internet protocol addresses, and any unique identifiers such as social security numbers, account numbers, or vehicle identifiers. These identifiers might occur in metadata about the learner, and in the learner's text(s).

The SweLL project adopted a rather restrictive approach to metadata describing important aspects about each produced text and learner in a way that learners are de-identified while still providing important information for research purposes about the learner's gender, age, total time in Sweden, education level and languages spoken in various communicative situations. The full set of metadata will be described in Section 3.2.

De-identification through metadata might not be solely satisfactory, since the texts written by a learner may also contain personal information

---

[4]Information about anonymization approaches in other projects comes from personal communication with involved researchers

connected to the learner, see for example Figure 1 where metadata in combination with the text may give away the physical person behind them. This means that we need to manipulate the text written by the learner with the purpose of hindering the possibility of going back to the original text, e.g. mention of profession *web developer* in Figure 1 to guarantee that the learner is de-identified.

SOCIO-DEMOGRAPHIC METADATA

- L1: Romansh, German, Korean

- Year of birth: 2001

- Gender: male

- Education / highest degree: high school

- Time in L2 country: 1 year

- Other languages: Russian, French

TASK METADATA:

- Date: April 2018

- CEFR level: A2

TEXT: "My name is Ali and I live in Växjö. I am 17 years. I moved to Sweden one year ago. I like Växjö. I am web developer."

Figure 1. Example of (selected) metadata and an essay text for a fake learner.

Since we need to keep the information about the learner throughout the project in order to be able to delete his/her record in the database if the learner so requests, we pseudonymize (rather than anonymize) both the text and the information about the learner. How we handle the identification of personal information and pseudonymization in learners' texts is described in detail in Section 3.3.

3.1 Data management in SweLL

The processing of SweLL data—from collection through storing to search and retrieval—is based on the ethical frontier *Building digital trust: The role of data ethics in the digital age*, developed by Accenture labs (Accenture, 2016), which describes best practices for data sharing. The model for the SweLL project data handling process is based upon this seven-step model (as described by *Data ethics and digital trust*). The model includes i) acquisition, ii) storing, iii) aggregation iv) analysis v) usage, vi) sharing and vii) disposal. Here, we give a brief outline to this process.

During *data collection* the teachers inform learners of the project and its aims. To ensure that the learners understand what they agree to we provide information not only in Swedish but also in several other languages common as mother tongues (L1) among learners of Swedish, including Arabic, Bosnian-Croatian-Serbian, Dari, English, Farsi, Greek, Kurmanji, Sorani, Somali, Spanish and Tigrinya[5]. In the consent, we inform the learners about the project, and describe the management of personal information throughout the project, including the statement that participation is entirely voluntary and the subject can opt out of continued involvement whenever he/she wants without the need to provide any explanation. Further, we state that we will not disclose the person's name and we will remove personal information from the texts to guarantee anonymity. Since the agreement covers a period of a learner's involvement in the project (e.g. a year) which is stated in the agreement, we do not need to ask for a new agreement every time we collect a text from a learner.

Once the learner agreed to donate his or her text(s) to the project, the teachers are responsible for the collection of the essays and additional personal- and task-specific metadata about the learner, the assignment, and the learner's grade. For each learner, we collect 1) the agreement form signed by the learner and 2) personal information about the learner. From each teacher, we collect 1) information about the assignment, and 2) the learner's grade of a particular essay when applicable. We collect agreements and metadata forms from the learners under teachers' guidance (in some cases in the presence of researchers or project assistants).

Data and data-related documents are handled and stored, making them both secure and easily accessible within the project for further processing. Teachers keep agreements, metadata sheets, task sheets and hand-written essays in safes at their schools until the documents are collected by researchers/project assistants. In the case of electronic essays, they are copied to a USB-memory stick and kept in a safe. Once the data and all related documents are transported by the project assistants/researchers from schools, all agreements

---

[5]However, as a word of warning—to ensure that project assistants can interpret the filled forms correctly, subjects usually fill in the Swedish form, and use translations only as support.

are collected and stored (on paper) in a safe.

To hide the identity of the learner for each essay, we assign a SweLL-ID to each learner. The SweLL-ID is inserted into the personal metadata sheet's special field. Project assistants register the personal metadata on the SweLL portal creating a "learner"-record. The list with the mappings between the learner's name and SweLL-ID is defined as *the key*. The key is kept in a safe, together with agreements, metadata sheets and the hand-written essays. The key is necessary to be kept making it possible to delete learner specific data if a participating subject (individual) so requests.

Information about the assignment provided by the teachers is uploaded to a portal by creating a task-ID, which is then linked to relevant essays. Where there are handouts, they are scanned and saved to the "task" profile. The forms containing information about the assignment are delivered either on a USB-memory stick or on paper.

The essays written by the learners are processed by researchers and research assistants. The essays originally written on computer as non-anonymized are saved on USB-memory and kept in a safe. On upload of an essay, the essay is linked to the specific SweLL-ID (with the learner's personal metadata). The handwritten essays are transcribed by project assistants using encrypted portal functionalities (SweLL-kiosk mode). All the essays written by the same person are connected systematically through the SweLL-ID and metadata information without revealing the identity of the learner.

Within the project, we operate under GDPR for the essay collection and pseudonymization. Neither the participating learners', nor the teachers' identity are to be revealed to the public. However, the list of participating teachers and schools, and the list of participating subjects with their SweLL-IDs are kept throughout the project in a safe to secure contact information in the long-term during the entire project period. Once the data is de-identified and the texts are pseudonymized, the data is made available to the public with a restricted license, which requires login and password for access to the portal.

3.2 Pseudonymization in metadata in SweLL

When designing the set of metadata, we tried to strive for necessary and detailed information for research purposes without jeopardizing the identi-

fication of the learners. Metadata concerning personal information about the learners is required for the project purpose to develop methods and exercises to particular groups of learners with various first and second languages, language skills and grades.

Personal metadata includes information about the learner's gender (<female>, <male>, <decline to respond/other>); instead of exact year of birth or age, the date of birth is given in 5-year interval spans (e.g. 1950–1954); instead of arrival date to Sweden, we ask for total time in Sweden in years and months; no information is provided on the educational establishment where the essays have been collected, but we ask for education level outside and in Sweden in years (<elementary school>, <introductory programme>, <gymnasium/upper secondary school>, <technical/vocational school>with degree, <university/other inst. of higher education>with degree and <other>. To further complicate possible identification of a learner through aggregated personal information, the metadata does not provide a country of origin or nationality of the learner but we restrict to information about the mother tongue (L1) only. Lastly, we ask information about how the learner learned Swedish (self-taught or took Swedish courses given as number of years and months).

In order to ensure high quality and usefulness of the corpus in research and development, information about the writing task is also essential, represented as additional task-oriented metadata without any personal information about the learner. We also ask teachers to provide the grade or result of the exercise for each particular essay written by each learner; For identification the learner's SweLL-ID is assigned instead of the name of the learner.

3.3 Pseudonymization of texts in SweLL

For the SweLL data set of the texts written by the learners, we manually identified text segments that reveal personal information in a subset of the corpus data. The following named entity types with sub-types were identified :

- Personal name: including <first_name>, <middle_name>, and <surname>. *Descriptor*: GENDER: <male>, <female>, <unknown>; CASE: <genitive>; INITIALS: in case of initials <ini>.

- Institution: referring to schools, working places, sport team, etc. *Descriptor*: <school>, <work>, <other_institution>.

- Geographic data: country, city, Swedish city, region, geographical areas (e.g. forest, lake, mountain), areas (e.g. city areas, municipalities), street, number (e.g. of building), zip code,

- Transportation: <transport>(e.g. subway, train, bus), <transport_line>(e.g. line no. 3, or green line)

- Age: the person's age given as a random number from a 5-year interval (age:FROM-TO) (e.g. 20 given as age: 18-22)

- Dates: elements directly related to an individual: <day>, <month_digit>expressed as digit (e.g. 5), <month_word>expressed as word (e.g. May), year <FROM–TO>given as a five-year span (e.g. 2018 as 2016–2020).

- Phone numbers: <phone_nr>

- Email addresses: <email>

- Personal web pages: <url>

- Social security numbers: <personid_nr>

- Account numbers: <account_nr>

- Certificate/licence numbers (e.g. vehicle): <license_nr>

- Profession: the person's profession <prof>, or the person's education <edu>

- Sensitive information that might reveal physical and mental disabilities, political views, unique family relations such as a large number of siblings, etc. <sensitive>

- Extra: any other items that are not covered by the previous categories. Distinction is made between objects that need to be replaced because of sensitivity *oblig*, and objects that might be sensitive but can be replaced later *nonoblig*

The list is not exhaustive, and we expect to refine the identified types above as we manually add more texts to the corpus.

Since we want to be able replace the information in the same morphological form as the original written by the learner, morphological features are also added to text strings containing personal information. These include Case: genitive <gen>, Form: definiteness <def>, and Number: <plural>. However, noteworthy that we do not keep track of spelling errors during pseudonymization as these are difficult to replicate in a pseudonymized version.

To keep the information about named entities with the same reference, each unique type (e.g. name or city) gets its own running number, starting with 1. If the particular word is repeated in the text, the same running number is assigned to it.

In the SweLL project, data—where possible—is pseudonymized in two steps: first we mark-up the text string containing personal data token by token on the basis of the named entity types by using a placeholder to keep track of which tokens in the text have been changed; then we replace the marked text string (i.e. placeholder) either by rendering, or by replacement with another token of the same named entity type. In some cases, when the annotator does not know how to categorize a certain text string, the original text is kept but marked by the placeholder, see Figure 2:

1. ORIGINAL TEXT → @PLACEHOLDER →RENDERING
2. ORIGINAL TEXT → @PLACEHOLDER →REPLACEMENT
3. ORIGINAL TEXT → @PLACEHOLDER →ORIGINAL

Figure 2. Pseudonymization steps, three ways to handle personal information, the SweLL approach.

Thus, pseudonymization consists of two distinct steps: 1. first marking up (i) information that directly or indirectly can reveal the author as well as (ii) sensitive information about the author, using @*placeholders*, and then
2. replacing the @*placeholders* by rendering or replacement.

Figure 3 illustrates an example of the pseudonymization tool where the male first name 'Ali' 'firstname:male_1' is identified (marked in red) and marked up as 'firstname:male_1'. Then, the male name 'Ali' is replaced, randomly selected from a list of male names registered in Sweden, in this case by 'Peter'.

This two-step process potentially opens a possibility to set an essay into different cultural contexts, for example by selecting names and cities from a certain country or part of the world. The first case in Figure 2 (1), that is rendering, can be applied to the information that can be collected from general resource lists, such as personal names and surnames; city and country names, nationalities and languages; geographic names (lakes, mountains, regions, etc.); street names, names of schools, institutions, work places; etc.

However, we need to refine our approach even further, among other things, when it comes to different numerical types of information with different formatting where general resource lists cannot suffice. Thus, the second way of handling personal information, see Figure 2 (2), is replacement, and applies to the cases where we need to replace information directly during the pseudonymization phase. This covers the following cases:

- middle names and initials are replaced with an "A" for each token used in those names;

- all numerical information (dates, phone numbers, certificate/license numbers, etc) is replaced according to the pattern used in the original, preserving all delimiters, e.g. dates: 2018/01/01 →@DATE_DIGITS →1111/11/11 or phone numbers: 089-777-654-22 →@TEL_NR →000-000-000-00;

- age, both written in digits and in strings. We replace @age with a random number from the range of plus/minus two years from the number provided in the text, for instance a number between 16 and 20 if the original age is 18. However, the complicating moment here is that learners may write the age in strings and make an error with that, so that it needs to be interpreted first by an assistant, and second the number range needs to be provided for the tool to apply a random number selection, preserving only the @placeholder tag in the end. For example:

[ORIGINAL] MY ELDER SISTER IS THIRTY AND MY YOUNGER SISTER IS *EITY.
→[CORRECTION] MY ELDER SISTER IS THIRTY AND MY YOUNGER SISTER IS EIGHTEEN (OR EIGHT ?).
→[@PLACEHOLDER + RANGE] MY ELDER SISTER IS @AGE_STRING(28-32) AND MY YOUNGER SISTER IS @AGE_STRING(16-20)

→[RANDOM REPLACEMENT] MY ELDER SISTER IS @AGE_STRING(28) AND MY YOUNGER SISTER IS @AGE_STRING(20)

The third case of handling personal information according to Figure 2 (3) is, in fact, a sub-case of (1), where rendering is not applied. In that case we are marking up a text segment, but do not take any actions until further notice (or rather decision). This covers cases where it is not clearcut whether the information may be considered risky to keep or not. Consider the following examples:

- professions: *I am a web developer.*

- education: *I am taking courses in Linguistics.*

- political or religious views: *We were happy to participate in a demonstration against Erdogan.*

- number of siblings or family members: *I have five sisters and three brothers.*

The different approaches across various learner corpus projects have their advantages and disadvantages. By manually replacing the learner text with strings like *Adam* or *Eva*, there is little chance that the general flow of text will be changed in an unwanted way, that is, the context, the morphological form and imitation of a learner error will be manually taken care of. The necessary prerequisite, then, is to keep track of the tokens that have been manipulated (i.e. not originally written by the learner) for potential post-pseudonymization purposes. However, the possibility of setting a learner text into a different context or other types of studies is lost. Also, they give rise to strings of the following type: *I have three sisters and four brothers. Their names are Eva, Eva and Eva, and Adam, Adam, Adam and Adam.*

In case of *@placeholders* of various kinds (including XML notation) that are preserved in the final text, the readability of the text is hampered, for instance *Hi, my name is @firstname:female_1, I live in @area_2 towards @area_3.* Besides, the possible errors that have been made by the learner are not reflected in this notation, e.g. *@area_2* was originally misspelled as *Stokhulm* (instead of Stockholm).

In case of *@placeholders* that are replaced automatically in the final version or rendered automatically on upload of an essay, on top of the previously described loss of error information, there is a non-negligible chance of

(1) introducing an error that was not originally made by a learner, e.g. *Ukrainians are ...* $\rightarrow$ *@nationality are ...* $\rightarrow$ *Swede are ...* where the pseudonymization has failed to preserve the plural form. Another example is *I worked in Charing Cross Hospital* $\rightarrow$ *I worked in @workplace* $\rightarrow$ *I worked in Volvo* where the preposition *in* sounds incorrect in a combination with Volvo as a company.

(2) not being able to preserve the forms that a learner has used, e.g. *Alice's wallet was stolen* $\rightarrow$ *@female_name wallet was stolen* $\rightarrow$ *Jane wallet was stolen* where the genitive form has not been automatically added and hence an error is introduced into the pseudonymized version. Even though the possessive form seems easy to be fixed, certain languages have rich inflectional morphology - which is impossible to reproduce unless a full morpho-syntactic tag (MSD) is added to the pseudonymized segment, something that makes the manual pseudonymization work by far more complex, error-prone and time-consuming, whereas projecting automatically assigned morpho-syntactic descriptors (MSDs) from automatically annotated original version might be non-straightforward and need further testing for reliability.

There is a trade-off between the benefits of adding the information on errors, MSDs, on lexical and syntactic restrictions (e.g. combinability with prepositions) and common knowledge (e.g. to avoid sequences like *I lived in Berlin, the capital of Venezuela*) and the increased time investment and error rate of doing that.

3.4 Pseudonymization tool in SweLL

During the pseudonymization phase, the research assistants work with essays on a special encrypted hard drive, *SweLL-kiosk*, designed for the purposes of transcription and pseudonymization. The environment does not allow any access to the internet except to a single url-address (i) for reporting technical issues and annotation considerations for discussion with other project members, (ii) for transferring the original essay to a secure data storage outside of anybody's—even project members'—reach and (iii) for transporting pseudonymized essays to an online database, from where any other authorized users can start working on normalization and annotation.

SweLL-kiosks contain a specially designed database and annotation management functionalities, that give an overview over the tasks at hand and completed tasks. On upload of new essays, they are tokenized, and in future we plan to test using full linguistic annotation to explore named entity recognition (NER) for support of anonymization, as well as to evaluate the relevance and benefits of projecting MSDs to the pseudonymized segments. During the work on pseudonymization, continuous versioning is enabled.

All personal information is marked up and masked according to the types described in Section 3.2, using the *SVALA tool* for pseudonymization (Rosén et al., 2018). SVALA links original text to the pseudonymized text building a parallel version with links going from one version to another, token by token. *@placeholder* tags are assigned to the links, as shown in Figure 3. The menu on the left shows a list of *@placeholder* tags, the menu on the right keeps track of unique *@placeholders*.

Data is stored in a JSON format, where information is kept about the source text, the target text, which segments have been manipulated, and the edges between the source and target segments. The edges are displayed as shown in Figure 4, describing the token *Borlänges* and its *@placeholder* label *city-SWE_2*.

To understand the de-identified and masked version of the essay, we keep track of references to the same persons and places, as we described in Section 3.2: if a unique name or place occurs more than once in the text, these are enumerated with the same number, and replaced by a unique pseudonym, as shown in the case of *Borlänge* in Figure 3 which is replaced by *Guntorp* in both places in the text.

The collected data is aimed for research scenarios of many kinds so we mask the absolutely necessary personal information only but without taking any risk of the possibility to identify the person behind the essay. This is not straightforward, and needs manual supervision. Even though we have named entity recognizers that can automatically detect names, places, or numeric expressions (phone numbers, street addresses) with high precision, learner data contains many spelling mistakes, and less well-formed sentences which make these tools less reliable. To guarantee anonymity, we carry out the identification and masking of personal information manually, sentence by sentence,

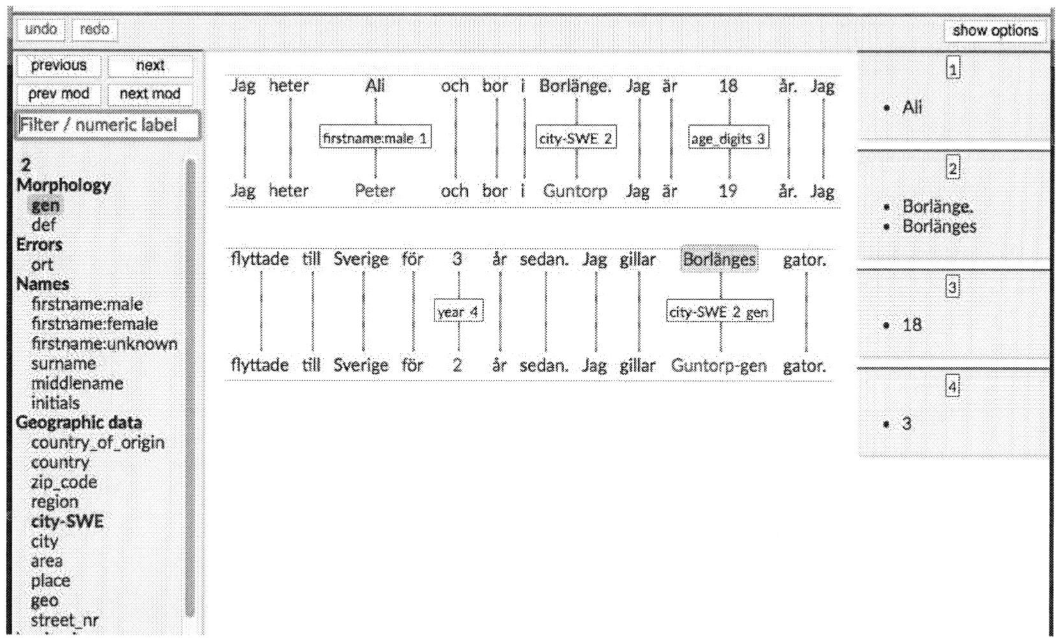

Figure 3: Example of pseudonymization in the SVALA tool.
Gloss-original: *My name is Ali and I live in Borlänge. I am 18 years old. I moved to Sweden 3 years ago. I like Borlänge's streets.* Gloss-pseudonymized: *My name is Peter and I live in Guntorp. I am 19 years old. I moved to Sweden 2 years ago. I like Guntorp's streets.*

essay by essay.

```
"e-s6-t49": {
  "id": "e-s6-t49",
  "ids": ["s6", "t49"],
  "labels": ["city-SWE", "2"],
  "manual": true
},
```

Figure 4: SVALA data format for edges.

In addition, the learners might write personal information in several essays which altogether might reveal the identity of the learner. To prevent such cases, we manually check all the essays written by a specific learner.

Once the text is pseudonymized, the de-identified essay is moved from the encrypted environment to the online SweLL portal for further processing, to normalize, correct and annotate the text accordingly.

4   Conclusions and future outlook

We presented on-going work on building a research infrastructure for Swedish as a second language with the focus on pseudonymization of learner essays. We described the legal issues influencing the way data needs to be handled and manipulated to ensure anonymity of data subjects, i.e. learners providing us with essays. This influences the way the data is collected, stored and pseudonymized. We gave an overview of the taxonomy for pseudonymization and presented the approaches and tools used for that.

The corpus is under development, as are the tools, and we envisage a number of experiments in order to

- add rendering functionality to our SVALA pseudonymization tool, and prepare resources that can be used for that,

- evaluate the necessary constraints—linguistic and extralinguistic—to ensure logical rendering, so that we do not get strings of the type *I lived in Berlin, the capital of Venezuela,*

- evaluate NER for support of manual pseudonymization, and

- evaluate projecting MSDs for keeping track of grammatical and orthographical choices made by learners.

We expect the corpus and the tools to be released as open source by the end of 2020.

To date there are no systematic studies that focus on the questions of the influence of pseudonymization of learner corpora on readability, text fluency, reader attitudes, assessment and annotation quality, or how it is best to render personal or potentially sensitive information. Nor does there seem to be tools that exploit automatic methods, e.g. Named Entity Recognition, for fully or semi-automatic learner text pseudonymization. All of which opens a whole new field for research.

Acknowledgements

We are very grateful to the two anonymous reviewers for useful comments and suggestions for improvements on the draft of our paper. This work has been supported by an infrastructure grant from the Swedish Foundation for Humanities and Social Sciences (Riksbankens Jubileumsfond: SweLL - research infrastructure for Swedish as a second language, project IN16-0464:1).

References

Accenture. 2016. *Building digital trust: The role of data ethics in the digital age.* `https://www.accenture.com/t20160613T024441__w__/us-en/_acnmedia/PDF-22/Accenture-Data-Ethics-POV-WEB.pdf`.

Malin Ahlberg, Lars Borin, Markus Forsberg, Martin Hammarstedt, Leif-Jöran Olsson, Olof Olsson, Johan Roxendal, and Jonatan Uppström. 2013. Korp and Karp - a bestiary of language resources: the research infrastructure of Språkbanken. In *Proceedings of the 19th Nordic Conference of Computational Linguistics (NODALIDA 2013)*, pages 429–433.

Council of Europe. 2001. *Common European Framework of Reference for Languages: Learning, Teaching, Assessment.* Press Syndicate of the University of Cambridge.

Karën Fort. 2016. *Collaborative Annotation for Reliable Natural Language Processing: Technical and Sociological Aspects.* John Wiley & Sons.

Ben Medlock. 2016. An Introduction to NLP-based Textual Anonymisation. In *Proceedings of Language Resources and Evaliation*, pages 1051–1056.

Nives Mikelić Preradović, Monika Berać, and Damir Boras. 2015. Learner Corpus of Croatian as a Second and Foreign Language. In *Multidisciplinary Approaches to Multilingualism*. Peter Lang.

Riksdagen. 1949. *Tryckfrihetsförordningen (1949:105).* `http://www.riksdagen.se/sv/dokument-lagar/dokument/svensk-forfattningssamling/tryckfrihetsforordning-1949105_sfs-1949-105`.

Alexandr Rosen. 2017. Introducing a corpus of non-native Czech with automatic annotation. *Language, Corpora and Cognition*, pages 163–180.

Dan Rosén, Mats Wirén, and Elena Volodina. 2018. Error Coding of Second-Language Learner Texts Based on Mostly Automatic Alignment of Parallel Corpora. In *CLARIN Annual conference 2018*.

Kari Tenfjord, Paul Meurer, and Knut Hofland. 2006. The ASK corpus: A language learner corpus of Norwegian as a second language. In *Proceedings of the 5th International Conference on Language Resources and Evaluation (LREC)*, pages 1821–1824.

Elena Volodina, Lena Granstedt, Sofia Johansson, Beáta Megyesi, Julia Prentice, Dan Rosén, Carl-Johan Schenström, Gunlög Sundberg, and Mats Wirén. 2018. Annotation of learner corpora: first SweLL insights. In *Proceedings of SLTC 2018, Stockholm, Sweden*.

Elena Volodina, Beáta Megyesi, Mats Wirén, Lena Granstedt, Julia Prentice, Monica Reichenberg, and Gunlög Sundberg. 2016a. A Friend in Need? Research agenda for electronic Second Language infrastructure. In *Proceedings of SLTC 2016, Umeå, Sweden*.

Elena Volodina, Ildikó Pilán, Lars Borin, and Therese Lindström Tiedemann. 2014. A flexible language learning platform based on language resources and web services. In *LREC*, pages 3973–3978.

Elena Volodina, Ildikó Pilán, Ingegerd Enström, Lorena Llozhi, Peter Lundkvist, Gunlög Sundberg, and Monica Sandell. 2016b. Swell on the rise: Swedish learner language corpus for European reference level studies. *Proceedings of LREC 2016*.

Work Smart – Reducing Effort in Short-Answer Grading

Margot Mieskes
Hochschule Darmstadt, h_da
Darmstadt, Germany
`margot.mieskes@h_da.de`

Ulrike Padó
Hochschule für Technik Stuttgart, HFT
Stuttgart, Germany
`ulrike.pado@hft-stuttgart.de`

Abstract

In language (and content) instruction, free-text questions are important instruments for gauging student ability. Grading is often done manually, so that frequent testing means high teacher workloads. We propose a new strategy for supporting manual graders: We carefully analyse the performance of automated graders individually and as a grader ensemble and present a procedure to guide manual effort and to estimate the size of the remaining grading error. We evaluate our approach on a range of data sets to demonstrate its robustness.

1 Introduction

Using computers in teaching has opened up new possibilities for learning independent of time or location while receiving individual feedback through frequent testing. For this, automated evaluation of student answers, supported most easily by closed question formats like multiple choice, is key. This means that tests usually do not contain open question types like short answer questions, although these are didactically valuable because they provide insight into students' reasoning.

There is a substantial body of research addressing automated short-answer grading (SAG, see Burrows et al. (2015) for an overview). However, the resulting tools are not widely used to produce completely automated student feedback. Instead, automated methods to reduce manual grading workload have been proposed (which can also be used to reduce annotation workload for training data in general). The use of clustering for label propagation (Basu et al., 2013; Horbach et al., 2014; Zesch et al., 2015; Horbach and Pinkal, 2018) and of Active Learning (Horbach and Palmer, 2016) has been investigated.

In this paper, we describe a new strategy to reduce human graders' workloads. We pre-grade student answers with automated methods that have been carefully analysed to reveal their strengths and weaknesses with regard to the target categories. Combining several automated graders into an ensemble additionally yields insight into the reliability of individual machine grades. Human grading effort can now be focused on reviewing those answers that were most likely not graded correctly.

Effectively, we harness two basic insights of machine learning: Learners perform best on frequently-attested classes (and consequently, under-represented classes require more human attention), and ensembles of learners outperform any given single model (and consequently, automated decisions with high agreement across learners are likely reliable).

Our strategy allows a sizeable reduction of human effort (by at least 40% and up to 93%), while grading accuracy remains at or even improves beyond purely human grading.Since not every student answer is reviewed by a teacher, our approach does not support individual teacher comments on each answer. It is useful in situations where overall performance is being determined by accumulating the grades for individual answers, for example placement tests or recurring text comprehension tests.

Our paper is structured as follows: We first give an overview over related work in manual grader support for SAG (Section 2). We then describe our method and our seven data sets, the machine learning algorithms and features, as well as the evaluation measures in Section 3. In Section 4, we analyse human grading performance in terms of Precision, Recall and Inter-Annotator Agreement to establish a point of comparison. We then investigate the strengths and weaknesses of an automated

Margot Mieskes and Ulrike Padó 2018. Work smart – Reducing effort in short-answer grading. *Proceedings of the 7th Workshop on NLP for Computer Assisted Language Learning at SLTC 2018 (NLP4CALL 2018).* Linköping Electronic Conference Proceedings 152: 57–68.

grader compared to the human gold standard (Section 5). In Section 6, we assess how much grading effort can be saved and how much grading error remains when we use reliability estimates that are based on the Inter-Annotator Agreement of machine grades only. We summarise our conclusions and point out future work in Section 8.

2   Related Work

Recent work in minimising human annotation effort for short-answer questions has followed two strategies: Clustering similar answers so that each set can be graded together (Basu et al., 2013; Brooks et al., 2014; Horbach et al., 2014; Zesch et al., 2015) or existing grades can be propagated (Horbach and Pinkal, 2018), and selecting the most informative answers for Active Learning (Horbach and Palmer, 2016). Manual workload is reduced either in order to directly benefit teachers (Basu et al., 2013; Horbach et al., 2014; Horbach and Pinkal, 2018) or in order to assist the creation of training data for automatic grading (Zesch et al., 2015; Horbach and Palmer, 2016).

Beyond faster grading, clustering similar answers can also provide interesting insights into common (mis-)perceptions of the subject matter according to Basu et al. (2013), which underscores the didactic usefulness of short-answer questions. In follow-up work, Brooks et al. (2014) demonstrate a speed increase for assigning an initial grade of a factor of three when using clustering support (which corresponds to 66% of time saved). They work on native-speaker content-assessment data, while Horbach et al. (2014) develop a similar approach for language learner data and report a comparable speedup: Using their method could save the correction of 60% of items at 85% grading accuracy. Horbach et al. (2014) acknowledge that perfect scoring accuracy is not necessary in many testing settings; we will investigate human performance levels in Section 4 below. Zesch et al. (2015) aim to reduce the amount of manual annotation required to create training data for automated graders and find that the clustering approach is most useful for very short answer texts.

Horbach and Palmer (2016) perform Active Learning, where instances to be manually labelled are selected to quickly optimise classifier performance. They find that uncertainty-based sample selection is more efficient in improving the classifier than a random and a cluster-based baseline.

However, there is great performance variability across the question corpus.

Zesch and Horbach (2018) introduce a clustering and classification workbench intended to facilitate both first practical applications of human grader support and further research.

3   Experimental Setup

Our experiments target ad-hoc tests such as weekly quizzes or end-of-term exams, where question re-use is limited. This sets us apart from approaches that use a corpus of sample answers to prepare grading models for a standardised question pool. Rather, it restricts us to an unseen-question setting in which no training answers are available for any of the questions in the test set. We use various data sets (Section 3.1) to train machine learners (Section 3.2) and evaluate their performance using Precision/Recall and Inter-Annotator Agreement (IAA) (Section 3.3).

3.1   Data

We test the generality of our findings by using a range of standard corpora that vary in size, language and test setting (see Table 1). Our largest corpus is ASAP, although only five out of ten questions have a reference answer and can be used in the unseen question setting. Five corpora are in English, two in German. Half of our corpora are collections of questions generated for low-volume testing (of tens of students at a time) that are graded by the teachers. SEB, Beetle and ASAP (Higgins et al., 2014) are from high-volume, standardised testing and grading situations. Both corpora of language learner data (CREG and CREE) fall into this category; the other corpora test content mastery. For four data sets (ASAP, CREE, CSSAG and Mohler) we have more than one set of human annotations.[1]

We also show the number of grade categories present in each corpus.[2] We generally observe a strong skew towards the majority category in our multi-class corpora. These characteristics of the data will be relevant in Sections 4 and 5 below.

---

[1] CREG also has multiple annotations, but was constructed to contain only answers with agreeing human annotation.

[2] We use the unseen question, two-way versions of the SEB and Beetle training data.

Corpus	#Questions/ #Answers	# Classes (% max class)	Language	Task	Human Annotation	Testing Volume
ASAP (www.kaggle.com/c/asap-sas)	5/8182	5 (46%)	EN	Content	Double	high volume
SEB (Dzikovska et al., 2013)	135/4969	2 (60%)			Single	
Beetle (Dzikovska et al., 2013)	47/3941	2 (58%)			Single	
Mohler (Mohler et al., 2011)	81/2273	11 (49%)			Double	low volume
CREE (Meurers et al., 2011a)	61/566	2 (72%)		Language	Double	
CREG (Meurers et al., 2011b)	85/543	2 (50%)	GER		Double	
CSSAG (Padó and Kiefer, 2015)	31/1926	9 (38%)		Content	Double (subset)	

Table 1: Corpus sizes and characteristics

3.2 Automated Graders and Features

We follow the most common literature conceptualisation and treat the prediction of human short-answer grades as a classification task: The human grades are ordinal in nature, which means the order of the categories is defined, but the distance between individual categories is not. We normalise the categories by using the percentages of the maximum score (e.g., 0% and 100% for the two-category corpora). This is useful because questions can have different maximum scores, which means that the impact of absolute points differs across the corpus (2 points could be partially correct for one question, but fully correct for another). Of course this also means that some of the intermediate percentage-based categories will be rare (e.g., 33% will only occur for the subset of 3-point questions if grading is in one-point steps).

As four out of seven corpora have little data, which reduces the possibility to tune parameters, we follow recommendations by Madnani et al. (2016) and employ Random Forest (RF) and Support Vector Machines (SVM), adding Decision Trees (DT) as a third algorithm for their ease of interpretation (all from the Weka machine learning toolkit[3]).

Individual models are trained by leave-one-question-out cross-validation to make the most of our smaller data sets. We experimented with further parameter tuning on the Beetle and SEB data sets, which provide unseen-question dev and test sets. Tuning did improve performance on the test sets, but rarely affected performance in the leave-one-question-out setting. By Occam's razor, we therefore do not further tune parameters. This also applies to modifications of the training regime such as cost-sensitive learning. As a result, our learner performance underestimates the tuned, optimal case.

We use the feature set described by Padó (2016),

who selected representative features explored in the literature: N-Gram features (token and lemma-based), text similarity features (with/without stop words), the overlap between student and reference answer in terms of dependency parse and deep semantic representations, and textual entailment (decision and confidence).

3.3 Evaluation Measures

We report weighted **Precision** (P) and **Recall** (R)[4] – on the whole corpus in Section 4, for comparison to human performance; and per predicted category (see Section 5), for a more detailed performance analysis. P and R indicate how reliable a learner's category predictions are and how well they overlap with the actual incidence of that category. Note that weighted overall Recall corresponds to overall **Accuracy**. Overall weighted Recall Rec is computed as in Equation 1.

$$Rec = \frac{\sum_c \frac{TP_c}{TP_c + FN_c} * N_c}{N_{total}} \qquad (1)$$

Since $TP_c + FN_c = N_c$,

$$Rec = Acc = \frac{\sum_c TP_c}{N_{total}}. \qquad (2)$$

The advantage of Inter-annotator Agreement (IAA) measures such as **Fleiss' κ** ((1971), which is more general than Cohen's κ (1960)) is that they take into account chance agreement by considering the study-specific distribution of annotation categories. Fleiss' κ allows us to compute agreement for individual answers as well as on the question level. κ estimates the annotation reliability in cases where two or more annotators (human or machine) are present. It is computed as

$$\kappa = \frac{\bar{P} - \bar{P}_e}{1 - \bar{P}_e} \qquad (3)$$

---

[3] https://www.cs.waikato.ac.nz/ml/weka

[4] We do not report F_1 scores, as they are most useful to compactly compare overall classifier performance, while we are most interested in individual, class-based performance.

where $1 - \bar{P}_e$ denotes the agreement predicted by chance and $\bar{P} - \bar{P}_e$ denotes the agreement actually attained. $\bar{P}$ and $\bar{P}_e$ are calculated as:

$$\bar{P} = \sum_{i=1}^{N} \frac{P_i}{N} \qquad (4)$$

$$\bar{P}_e = \sum_{j=1}^{k} p_j^2 \qquad (5)$$

For each answer that receives a grade, we can calculate the individual agreement P_i as

$$P_i = \frac{\sum_{j=1}^{k} n(n_{ij} - 1)}{m(m-1)} = \frac{\sum_{j=1}^{k} n_{ij}^2 - n_{ij}}{m^2 - m} \qquad (6)$$

where m is the number of annotators, n_{ij} is the number of annotators that chose a category j for token i, k the number of categories and N the number of tokens.

We follow Yannakoudakis and Cummins (2015) and do not report correlation measures like Pearson's r and Spearman's ρ, as they are not appropriate for data with many ties (such as grading data sets with their fixed range of categories). Furthermore, r is sensitive to outliers, while ρ inherently measures the ability of a system to rank answers appropriately, as opposed to predicting the correct category. As such, correlation measures do not support our goal of determining how reliable item-wise machine predictions are.

4 Experiment 1: Comparing Human and Machine Performance

Our first experiment investigates human-human performance and compares it to the reliability of automated grading. We compute human P, R and κ for the data sets where informative double manual annotations are available (ASAP, CREE, CSSAG and Mohler). For the human data, we report the performance of the best single annotator against the gold labels and show machine P and R for comparison. We begin with the easiest setting: binary *correct-incorrect* classification for all corpora (where *correct* means $> 50\%$ of the max score). Results are shown in Table 2.

Human P/R results (H P and H R in Table 2) are in the eighties (up to 94 for ASAP) throughout. For the Mohler data, we show two performance numbers: For this data set, the gold standard is created by averaging the two single annotations; therefore, every annotator's grades are

highly correlated with the gold. This leads to artificially inflated P and R values (shown in brackets in Table 2). For the other grades, the gold standard was created independently (CSSAG) or one annotator's grades are marked as the gold standard (CREE and ASAP), so that the other's grades are independent of gold. Treating the Mohler data in this way (using annotator "me" as gold annotation) results in performance in the low eighties. We refer to this evaluation method als *Mohler strict evaluation* below.

Our results show that human annotation with up to 16.5% of error (Mohler strict evaluation, 14.2% for CREE) has been accepted in the past for low-volume testing. (Assuming error to be 1-Accuracy, that is 1-R, since weighted R equals Accuracy). For high-volume testing (ASAP), we see much lower rates at 6% error.

Human κ values vary widely across corpora and range from 0.41 (Mohler) to 0.82 (ASAP). The higher κ, the better the human annotators agreed on the grades, producing clearly defined categories and clean training data.

We find low κs for corpora collected as a by-product of low-volume, ad hoc testing with many different questions and different grade categories (CSSAG, CREE and Mohler). ASAP, collected in a high-volume testing setting, is the opposite, since the reliability of multi-annotator grading is a priority when single-annotator grading is impossible due to testing volume. Consequently, there is a small number of grade categories and clear scoring rubrics exist for each question (and graders were likely carefully trained to apply them consistently).

We present machine P and R for the RF learner, our best individual machine grader. It outperforms literature results from Padó (2016) (who used the same features). The SVM and DT learners show similar result patterns as RF, but perform an average of 3 (SVM) and 4 (DT) percentage points worse. Machine results are worse than human results except for the CREE corpus and also outperform the strict Mohler human-human P and R values (see above). Note that both these corpora are strongly skewed towards one class (87% and 72% of the items, respectively). In CSSAG (as well as in SEB and Beetle), the class balance moves to 60-40 and learner performance is noticeably worse. In fact, human P/R results for CSSAG are the strongest among the low-volume corpora, but

Proceedings of the 7th Workshop on NLP for Computer Assisted Language Learning at SLTC 2018 (NLP4CALL 2018)

Measure		ASAP	CREE	CREG	CSSAG	Mohler	Beetle	SEB
H	P	93.7	86.0	n.a.	89.2	82.7 (95.4)	n.a.	n.a.
	R	93.7	85.8	n.a.	89.9	83.5	n.a.	n.a.
RF	P	86.0	85.4	84.6	71.0	87.5 (93.6)	78.4	70.6
	R	86.2	86.0	84.5	70.4	89.0	78.0	70.7
H	κ	0.82	0.64	n.a.	0.54	0.41	n.a	n.a.

Table 2: Weighted Precision (P) and Recall (R): Human-gold (H) and machine-gold (Random Forest, RF) performance for binary classification. Human-human Fleiss' κ. n.a.: Single human annotation only.

the machine results are the lowest of all four corpora. This may be caused by the low reliability of the human annotations (evidenced by low κ). The strong skew of the Mohler data (49% of data points are annotated with the highest of 11 categories) probably masks a similar effect for that corpus.

5 Experiment 2: Strengths and Weaknesses of Single-Model Grading

Experiment 1 has presented human annotation standards and the performance of a vanilla automated grading model. While the automated grader clearly has room for improvement, our next analyses show that even unreliable machine predictions can considerably reduce human grading effort.

Our goal is to focus the human grading effort on those answers where it is most needed. We accept the consequence that not every student answer will be reviewed by a human grader and that some errors will remain in the final grades. Therefore, the approach is most suitable for testing situations where the grades for individual answers are combined into an overall grade. This accumulated grade is more robust towards some remaining error.

Note that the notion of "most needed human attention" depends on the testing context. In formative feedback situations, it is more acceptable to receive approximate grades than in high-stakes testing, since no decisive consequences depend on formative feedback. We will further discuss these issues below, where we strive to present the trade-off between grading accuracy and grading effort in order to allow users to find the ideal balance for their situation.

In this Section, we take a first step and discuss how to identify reliable machine grades based only on the RF grader's strengths and weaknesses. In Section 6, we will move on to comparing automated predictions from several learners for improved reliability estimates.

	Correct		Incorrect		Majority
Corpus	P	R	P	R	class
ASAP	69.8	66.3	90.6	91.9	I
CREE	89.8	93.1	68.0	57.9	C
CREG	83.3	85.2	85.8	84.1	–
CSSAG	54.3	58.3	79.1	76.3	I
Mohler	89.4	99.2	74.2	16.4	C
Beetle	70.8	76.5	83.4	78.9	I
SEB	70.0	52.7	70.9	83.7	I

Table 3: Weighted P and R per category (binary classification) and majority class (CREG is balanced by design). RF classifier.

5.1 Case 1: Binary classification

Table 3 shows category-wise P and R for binary classification. As can be expected, the majority class is predicted more reliably and with fewer errors in all cases. As CREG is balanced by design, there is no such frequency effect. For the highly imbalanced data sets, R drops steeply in the minority category (between 25%-points for ASAP – 71% incorrect – and 83%-points for Mohler – 87% correct) as the machine grader over-generalises to the majority category.

These results indicate that in a binary setting, manual effort should focus on reviewing the predicted minority class results, as the majority class is fairly reliably marked. For a strongly skewed corpus like ASAP, 1717 instances out of 8182 (21%) need to be reviewed, while for a less skewed corpus such as Beetle, 1708 out of 3942 instances (43%) need to be checked.

Since most corpora are imbalanced, checking only the minority class predictions would save 60-80% of labor while eliminating the largest error source. However, when relying on automatic graders, the information about which answers may have wrongly received the majority class is not available. Additionally, due to the binary setting, no additional information is available to reduce the error further.

In the case of low minority class recall in a high stakes situation, the risk of wrongly-assigned "pass" or "fail" grades is high. This means that all majority class predictions or at least a sample should additionally be checked to catch misassigned minority class answers.

5.2 Case 2: Multi-class classification

We now move on to the more complex multi-class case (where a spectrum of grades is assigned instead of just pass/fail). We have three data sets with more than two target categories: ASAP (five categories), CSSAG (nine) and Mohler (11). We again evaluate RF classification using P/R. We also report category-wise human-human performance for comparison.

Table 4 shows results for the CSSAG data. Clearly, in the harder multi-class case, both human and machine grader performance degrade compared to the results in Table 2. Recall that the human-human data is for a subset of CSSAG – there are additional categories in the whole data set that are not covered in the subset. Human performance on all metrics is best for the categories 0 and 1, with similar κ for 0.5. For categories 0.25 and 0.75, human agreement becomes erratic, with low P/R and κs, which indicates that these categories are not assigned consistently. This implies that these intermediary categories are not well-defined in the annotators' minds, which in turn causes data quality to suffer. Not surprisingly, therefore, the RF P and R show patterns of frequency (rare categories not attested in the human-human subset are predicted badly) and of annotation cleanness. Therefore, predictions of 0, 0.75 (high P) and 1 (which make up 74% of the training data) can be trusted, while the other 25% of predictions should be checked. Additional spot checks of 1 predictions are also advisable due to the lower P in high-stakes settings, while in formative settings, it may not be as important to differentiate between the fine-grained grade steps and over-generalisations to 1 may be acceptable.

Table 5 shows the results for ASAP. Again, both human and machine overall performance drop for the harder task, but with just five categories, the drop is not as steep. Also, human and machine performance is much more robust across all categories. The automated grader performs worst on categories 0.33 and 0.66. Since human performance is stable for these categories, this is probably a frequency issue as the categories are well-defined and clear to the annotators, and the automatic grader is generally reaping the benefits of

clean data for the majority class. The machine predictions for category 0, which makes up about half of the gold annotations, can generally be trusted, while predictions of 0.33 and 0.66 (23% of the data) should always be checked.

For the Mohler data set with 11 categories, the drop in performance from the binary classification case is clearest (Table 6, "overall" column; we present the stricter evaluation of one human annotator against the other). Looking at the category-wise results, the Mohler data set, like CSSAG, suffers from both ill-defined and sparsely attested categories. We see low human P/R except for 0 and 1 and low human κ except for 0.4, 0.6 and 1. Additionally, in case of human disagreement the difference between the human grades is often in the range of just one grade; this begs the question whether the difference between the 11 categories can in fact be reliably annotated. The data sparseness stems from the fact that the majority of questions uses only six categories. This results in no machine predictions or very low P/R except for categories 0 and 1.

Together, these two categories make up 50% of the training data. Any other category predictions are likely to be incorrect and should be checked; in a high stakes setting, even predictions for 1 could be additionally reviewed because the relatively low P at high R indicates over-generalisation towards this category.

In sum, when using a single, imperfect machine grader, we can already identify a relatively large set of student answers that is likely graded correctly and probably does not need further human attention. The more target categories there are in the data, the more fine-grained the analysis becomes, but also the reliability of both human and machine grades suffers. Therefore, in a high stakes situation, human graders can be most reliably supported by automated grades for a binary pass/fail decision if the machine grader shows high recall for the minority class. If this is not the case or if the distinction between more grade steps matters, the setup presented here may still be useful for formative feedback since repeated, formative feedback is a large drain of human grader resources and human time saved may outweigh the approximate nature of the grades.

As we use various data sets from a range of scenarios, our conclusions should be generalizable.

		Overall	0	0.17	0.25	0.33	0.5	0.66	0.75	0.83	1
H	P	77.2	79.2	–	62.5	–	57.4	–	39.1	–	93.5
	R	76.2	98.3	–	57.7	–	50.0	–	45.0	–	62.3
RF	P	49.1	63.7	0	18.2	0	40.7	15.8	75.0	0	38.4
	R	67.4	73.6	0	2.0	0	10.0	10.3	2.6	0	71.6
H	κ	0.54	0.65	–	0.27	–	0.59	–	0.36	–	0.68

Table 4: CSSAG: Human-gold (H) and machine-gold (RF) P and R, human-human κ values. – : No prediction made.

	Overall	0	0.33	0.5	0.66	1
H P	87.2	92.4	87.6	80.4	86.0	86.0
H R	87.2	92.4	86.6	81.3	86.0	85.1
RF P	64.7	81.8	39.3	61.8	34.2	47.6
RF R	67.4	89.0	23.9	64.4	22.8	64.5
H κ	0.82	0.88	0.86	0.74	0.85	0.82

Table 5: ASAP: Human-gold (H) and machine-gold (RF) P and R. Human-human κ values.

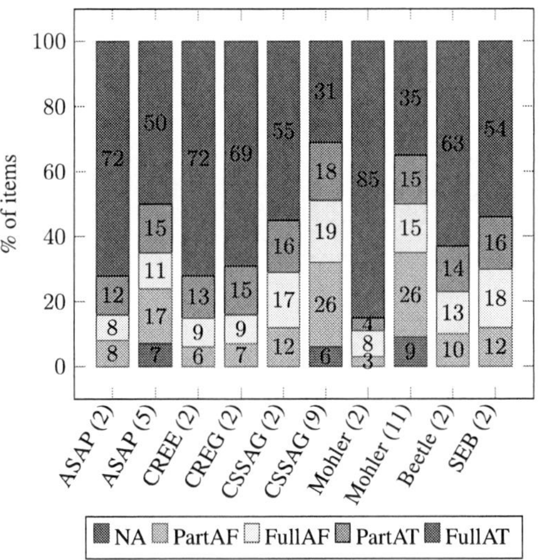

Figure 1: Proportion of items with no agreement (NA), partial agreement on false prediction (PartAF), full agreement on false prediction (FullAF), partial agreement on true prediction (PartAT) and full agreement on true prediction (FullAT), in brackets: # of classes.

6 Experiment 3: Item-wise Reliability of Ensemble Grading

We now switch from using a single automated grader to combining three automated graders (RF, DT and SVM). This approach allows us to generate multiple machine annotations and use them for reliability estimates. We use κ to analyse the automated graders' reliability down to the single-item level and to generate fine-grained reviewing recommendations for manual graders.

We assume that a machine grade is more reliable if more of the graders in our ensemble predict it (and therefore agree better, such that κ is high). With three learners, the item-wise predictions can be in full agreement (FullA, $\kappa = 1$), partial agreement (PartA, $\kappa = 0.83$) or no agreement (NA, $\kappa = 0$).

Figure 1 shows automated grader agreement and disagreement for the binary (and, where applicable) multi-class case. The number of target categories is given in brackets. This figure demonstrates that our assumption of *greater agreement = greater reliability* is generally justified: Compare the proportion of true and false predictions for full agreement and partial agreement. There are vastly fewer cases of FullAF (full agreement, false; yellow) than FullAT (full agreement, true; dark green), while cases of PartAF (partial agreement, false; orange) and PartAT (light green) are closer to balance.

Cases of FullAF (full agreement, false prediction; yellow) are generally around 10%, with a maximum of 19% for CSSAG (9). This is similar to human standards: Human annotators may also agree on a category that does not match the gold standard. In our CSSAG subset, this occurred for 10% of annotations, as well.

Given this picture, our recommendation is to manually review answers in the order of the amount of learner disagreement on the category, beginning with NA. The first lines of Table 7 show that in the binary case, reviewing only NA cases of course means no manual work (three graders have to agree at least partially on two labels, so there is always a clear majority for one label), at error levels between 11% (Mohler (2)) and 30% (SEB). For four out of the seven corpora, error levels would already be close to human agreement error (at $1 - Accuracy = 15\%$ – recall Section 4). This picture is close to single-grader performance in Section 5.1.

In the more complex multi-class case, this strategy reduces the manual grading effort to between 6% (CSSAG (9)) and 9% (Mohler (11)) of all items in the multi-class case. Assuming that the

		Overall	0	0.1	0.2	0.3	0.4	0.5	0.6	0.7	0.8	0.9	1
H	P	58.5	96.0	0	37.5	0	30.6	13.6	21.8	3.8	20.8	4.4	78.0
	R	57.3	19.0	4.4	0	0	1.0	13.6	23.8	25.0	27.4	8.7	86.3
RF	P	38.1	67.9	0	0	33.3	13.3	20.6	12.5	37.5	8.8	18.6	56.7
	R	50.9	95.0	0	0	2.9	2.2	5.7	5.8	13.8	2.4	6.7	94.9
H	κ	0.41	0.30	0.01	0.10	0.15	0.62	0.15	0.62	$\kappa < 0$	0.13	0.02	0.82
RF	κ	0.10	0.79	$\kappa < 0$	$\kappa < 0$	0.05	0.02	0.06	0.03	0.15	$\kappa < 0$	0.01	0.15

Table 6: Mohler: Human-gold (H) and machine-gold (RF) P and R. Human-human κ values. n.a.: No prediction made.

		Binary Classification							Multiclass		
Strategy	Measures	ASAP	CREE	CREG	CSSAG	Mohler	Beetle	SEB	ASAP	CSSAG	Mohler
NA	Effort (%)	0	0	0	0	0	0	0	7	4	9
only	Error (%)	16	**15**	16	29	**11**	23	30	28	44	41
PartA/	Effort (%)	12	7	–	12	5	13	12	23	35	50
weak	Error (%)	**12**	**13**	–	23	**9**	17	25	18	25	**15**
PartA/	Effort (%)	20	19	12	27	7	24	28	39	50	59
all	Error (%)	**8**	**9**	**9**	17	**8**	**13**	18	**11**	19	**15**

Table 7: Remaining effort (in % of items) and remaining error for all corpora following different review strategies. NA only: Review no-agreement answers; PartA/weak: Revise PartA predictions of classes with weak classifier performance; PartA/all: Revise all PartA predictions. **Bold**: Error **at** or **below** observed human agreement. –: CREG has no majority class.

hand-assigned categories are always correct, remaining error would then range between 28% (ASAP (5)) and 45% (CSSAG (9)). More human effort is clearly needed to further reduce error in most grading situations, even though grader workload has been greatly reduced over the single-grader case (where 25-50% of predictions had to be reviewed) and remaining error also drops for ASAP and Mohler compared to using a single grader.

Finding Errors Figure 1 implies that grades predicted in partial agreement are unreliable between 32% (CREE, CREG) and 43% (CSSAG (2), Mohler (2)) for the binary case and (at best) half of the time for the multiclass case. For comparison, grades predicted in full agreement are unreliable between 4 and 25% in the binary case and between 14 and 38% in the multiclass case. Focusing on PartA predictions is therefore an efficient use of human effort.

We can zoom in further on likely errors by concentrating on the categories that are most likely affected because the machine graders perform weakly on them. For ASAP (5), machine grading performance is known to be worst for classes 0.33, 0.66 and 1 (see RF performance in Table 5). 60% of the erroneous PA predictions are in fact for those classes. Reviewing all PartA cases for these categories, which make up 16% of the total data set, and additionally checking all items where the

machine graders disagree (7%) results in a reduction of manual grading effort of 77% of the items, while holding remaining error at 18%. Remaining error can be further reduced to 11% by revising the PartA predictions for *all* classes instead of just the weakest classes. Humans still review only 39% of all answers in this case (corresponding to 61% of effort saved).

Table 7 shows the remaining manual effort and error for all data sets for the PartA/weak strategy (revise cases of NA and those PartA categories that the RF grader is known to perform weakly on) as well as for the PartA/all strategy. For the binary corpora, the predictions for the minority class are reviewed for the PartA/weak strategy.

Clearly, the same patterns hold across all data sets: For binary classification, just using the ensemble predictions reaches error at human levels for CREE and Mohler (recall, however, that these corpora are strongly biased towards the majority class). When reviewing all PartA predictions, five out of seven corpora show remaining error levels below the observed human error level of 15%, and for four of these five, the error is even below 10% at a maximum of 28% of items reviewed. In the harder multiclass case, two of the three corpora show human-level remaining error, but some more reviewing effort is needed (up to 60% of items, or 50% for CSSAG at 20% remaining error). This mirrors the complexity of the task, but is still a sizeable reduction.

Relaxing the Evaluation A second measure that helps save human effort is reconsidering the gravity of machine errors in the multiclass case: In repeated formative testing, a difference between actual and predicted grade of one grade step out of five (or even eleven) may not be of much consequence for the student. To model this relaxed evaluation, we use the definitions from above for FullA, PartA and NA predictions. However, we now count a prediction as correct if it is within one grade step of the gold category. We also apply the relaxed prediction matching to the reviewing recommendations: We now only review NA cases and those PartA cases where the predictions differ by more than one grade step (the majority prediction is accepted for the other PartA cases).

This relaxation is very relevant: 75% of PartA predictions for the ASAP (5) data and 72% for the Mohler (11) data differ within one grade step. For CSSAG (9), however, only four out of more than 800 PartA predictions are within one grade step of another. This pattern of results can be explained by a tendency of the Decision Tree (DT) learner to predict the extreme categories. Since the Mohler and ASAP data are biased towards those categories, all the learners show this pattern and predictions match closely. CSSAG has a bias towards the middle category as well as the top that SVM and RF reflect better than DT. Therefore, they may cast votes that differ strongly from the DT vote.

The results of relaxed evaluation and review are very encouraging for practical application: For ASAP, error drops to 7% when reviewing just 25% of the data. This is at the human level observed for ASAP. Previously, reviewing all PartA predictions in strict evaluation, 11% of error remained and 38% of data were reviewed. For Mohler, 5% error remain after reviewing 38% of data (from 15% of error while reviewing 59% of data). For CSSAG, there is of course no change. This pattern of results makes the approach very promising for formative assessment, where testing is frequent (causing high grader workload) and the individual test result can still be informative even if it is approximate.

7 Implications for Real-World Users

Our motivation for this work was to help human graders in language instruction (and elsewhere) save time and effort on manual grading of free text answers. Our analysis shows that human effort can be reduced drastically by following our reliability-guided review strategy, while grading error stays at or even drops below the human level. However, there are a few points to consider for real-world graders as they choose the correct level of revision strictness for their testing context.

Human revision error We make the assumption that human review always determines the correct category. This may seem optimistic given the human error rate of up to 15% in Section 4, but it is hard to predict grader error more precisely for the general case. Our results in Section 4 show that grading error is lowest in a situation where graders have clear scoring rubrics and are (presumably) carefully trained. Ad hoc grading by teachers shows the highest error rates. For this scenario, it can be hoped that, as the number of answers to review drops, grader alertness and motivation will rise, leading to cleaner annotation. We therefore report the assumed-to-be-perfect numbers and leave it to each grader to discount them by the likely error rates incurred in their process.

Distortion of the grade distribution How will using the proposed method alter the grade distribution? The most conservative case means reviewing all PartA judgements, as this issue is likely to matter most when stakes are high. The only remaining system error (following our assumption about perfect human revisions) are the cases where the ensemble agrees on the wrong category. We analysed CSSAG multiclass, because it has multiple human annotations that are independent of gold (and therefore shows the phenomenon on humans agreeing on non-gold categories, like the machine ensembles). First of all, in both data sets (multiple human-annotated subset of CSSAG and multiple machine-annotated complete CSSAG), the most frequent categories are 0, 1 and 0.5, in this order. Another similarity is that in both cases, mis-assignments end up mostly in the more frequent classes. For the human annotations, mis-assignments are most often labelled 0 and 0.5, for the machine annotation, 0 and 1 (the two most frequent classes). There are, however, some differences: The humans showed a clear tendency to assign the next lower frequent class (mis-labelling 0.5 as 0 or 0.75 as 0.5). They rarely wrongly agreed on the label 1, and true 1s were labelled as 0.75 or even 0.5. Conversely, the machines are overly generous: They tend to mis-label as 1, even though 0 is the most frequent class in the data (almost twice as frequent as 1).The reason may be that many true 0 answers are simply empty or contain just a few (non-informative) words. The machines therefore tend to over-generalise to the next more frequent category, 1, if an answer does not fit that pattern, even if it is still incorrect. There is an indication of this behaviour in the learner performance in Table 4: Precision for class 1 is much lower than for class 0, at similar recall. This indicates that class 1 predictions are more often unreliable, and the machine is therefore being overly generous. Note, however, that this distortion affects only 11% of the data.

This error analysis suggests that we might improve the automated grader by training it only on non-empty incorrect answers, thereby removing the bias towards distinguishing between empty and non-empty rather than correct and incorrect. The empty answers would then be trivially labelled as incorrect after filtering.

In general, since items to review are chosen on the basis of classifier grades, if the ensemble shares a bias towards a specific category, the grades of that category will be reviewed disproportionally rarely. Fortunately, learner bias follows the frequency biases in the data, so that the bias categories are generally graded reliably, as mirrored in the remaining error levels for our strategy. However, classifier bias and it's tendency may still be relevant depending on the testing context, as we have seen.

Language lerner corpora In our experiments, language learner corpora generally fare better than content assessment corpora. The CREE and CREG corpora feature binary categories which were annotated reliably ($\kappa = 0.64$ for CREE, only items with annotator agreement for CREG). While a κ of 0.64 might not sound impressive, it gives an idea how hard the task of awarding the equivalent of "pass" or "fail" in these contexts are. This is the best-case scenario for the automated learners. In this situation, corpus size does not seem to matter as much as might be expected: The RF learner performs as well for CREE and CREG as it does for the binarised version of ASAP, which is roughly 16 times larger.

An additional factor in this scenario may be that CREE and CREG appear to be easier to machine-grade than many content-assessment corpora (Padó, 2016). Padó (2017) hypothesizes that this effect is due in part to the fact that the majority of questions in language learner corpora are text comprehension questions, which require reproduction and tend to produce answers that are very close to the reading text as well as the reference answer taken from this text. Additionally, language learners' limited proficiency may keep them from paraphrasing freely, which compounds the effect.

In sum, the language learner corpora we used for our experiments are very well suited to train reliable automated graders, and this is mirrored in the evaluation results: The machine ensemble predictions (in full and partial agreement) were correct at about the level of human performance (85% of labels correct) without any human review. This can optimally be raised to 91% correct categories when reviewing just 20% of the data. The remaining error (where the ensemble fully agrees on the wrong category) is at 9% of the data, which is the same level as human agreement on the wrong category for a subset of CSSAG.

This makes our strategy especially promising for free text grading in language instruction: On the one hand, the question type is frequent and grading therefore adds substantially to the teachers' workloads; on the other hand, machine-supported manual grading yields grades that are definitely reliable enough for formative testing and possibly even summative testing (after the reservations about possible distortions in grade distribution are considered).

Lessons for ad-hoc manual grading Comparing the CSSAG, Mohler and ASAP data set, we also observe that the amount of training data available per category and the quality of human annotation clearly matters. Although the categories are imbalanced in all data sets, the absolute number of examples for each of the five categories in the ASAP data is considerably higher than for Mohler and CSSAG, where some categories are very sparse. Also, the human κs are much higher and more consistent for the ASAP data. Consequently, the machine graders learn to make high-quality predictions. In light of this observation, we recommend using as few categories as possible in automatically supported grading to avoid sparseness issues and to prioritise clear category definitions (resulting in high human grader agreement). As the analysis of the manual grading shows, too many categories lead to unclear representations in humans as well, which in turn do not allow for clear models using machine learning. Fewer categories are also easier to interpret, as the differences of individual steps on a 10-point scale are less clear than differences for example on a 6-point scale.

In some NLP tasks, reducing the scale is not an option. Therefore, information about easily modelled categories could be used to focus the annotation effort on the harder categories to ensure consistent models.

8 Conclusions and Future Work

We have shown the practical usefulness of unoptimised automatic grading tools for reducing human grading effort, based on seven different corpora and two different grading scenarios. For the binary grading scenario, where only correct vs. incorrect is distinguished, effort can be reduced by at least 75%. In more complex grading scenarios of assigning grades based on various levels of granularity, effort can be reduced by at least 40% – depending on the scale complexity. This reduction in effort retains an acceptable error rate, which is comparable to or even below human error rate. In the literature reviewed in Section 2, a reduction in grading effort of of 60% is possible while the human error levels.

Although our suggested strategy involves various evaluation steps, it is nevertheless technically simple to use for the human grader: Individual automatic graders have to be analysed with respect to their performance using Precision and Recall in order to determine their biases. The automatic grader predictions are then compared using Inter-Annotator Agreement, which gives a detailed picture of the grading quality of individual categories and items. This enables the human grader to focus the correction effort on the most important cases, ignoring automatic annotations that are most likely correct.

The cases to be revised can be chosen according to available grading time and required level of remaining error: First, only items that did not receive an automatic grade have to be corrected. In the binary case this even means no manual effort at all, but this strategy also leaves the highest error rate. Second, only items where the automatic graders are not unanimous and predict weakly performing categories are manually checked. This re-

sults in an error rate of 9-25% while reviewing 13% of the data for the binary scenario and 25-50% of the data for the multiclass scenario. The most detailed strategy involves reviewing all items that did not receive an unanimous vote. This results in an error rate at or below human level, while reviewing 7-28% of the data for the binary scenario and 40-60% of the data for the multiclass scenario. Further reductions of effort and error are possible if evaluation is slightly relaxed in the multiclass case.

Our results match insights from the general machine learning domain: a) Grader performance correlates to the number of training instances for a category. b) By using three flawed automated graders, we make use of the power of error independence in the machine ensemble (Kuncheva, 2004).

Finally, based on our analysis we can give recommendations for Computer-Aided Language Learning (CALL), especially regarding the development of corpora, which serve as the basis of many approaches. In order to optimise machine grading performance, first, the grading scale should not be too fine-grained, as rarely occurring categories are problematic even for humans. Second, the grading categories should be clearly defined. But thirdly, even relatively small-sized corpora are sufficient to create good models for automatic pre-grading if the first two points are true.

Our strategy seems especially promising for short answer grading in language instruction. On the one hand, the question type is frequent and grading therefore adds substantially to the teachers' workloads; on the other hand, machine-supported manual grading in our experiments yields grades that are definitely reliable enough for formative testing at a fraction of the manual effort.

Given the encouraging results of the present study, a logical future step to extend this work would be a user study with real-world human graders, since our work so far has been carried out only on existing corpora.

References

Sumit Basu, Chuck Jacobs, and Lucy Vanderwende. 2013. Powergrading: a clustering approach to amplify human effort for short answer grading. *Transactions of the Association for Computational Linguistics (TACL)*, 1:391–402.

Michael Brooks, Sumit Basu, Charles Jacobs, and Lucy

Vanderwende. 2014. Divide and correct: Using clusters to grade short answers at scale. In *Proceedings of L@S '14,* Atlanta, Georgia, 4–5 March 2014, pages 89–98.

Steven Burrows, Iryna Gurevych, and Benno Stein. 2015. The Eras and Trends of Automatic Short Answer Grading. *International Journal of Artificial Intelligence in Education,* 25:60–117.

Jacob Cohen. 1960. A coefficient of agreement for nominal scales. *Educational and Psychological Measurement,* 20:37–46.

Myroslava Dzikovska, Rodney Nielsen, Chris Brew, Claudia Leacock, Danilo Giampiccolo, Luisa Bentivogli, Peter Clark, Ido Dagan, and Hoa Trang Dang. 2013. SemEval-2013 task 7: The joint student response analysis and 8th recognizing textual entailment challenge. In *Proceedings of SemEeval-2013,* Atlanta, Georgia, 14–15 June 2013, pages 263–274.

Joseph L. Fleiss. 1971. Measuring nominal scale agreement among many raters. *Psychological Bulletin,* 76(5):378–382.

Derrick Higgins, Chris Brew, Michael Heilman, Ramon Ziai, Lei Chen, Aoife Cahill, Michael Flor, Nitin Madnani, Joel R. Tetreault, Daniel Blanchard, Diane Napolitano, Chong Min Lee, and John Blackmore. 2014. Is getting the right answer just about choosing the right words? The role of syntactically-informed features in short answer scoring. *Computing Research Repository, Computation and Language.*

Andrea Horbach and Alexis Palmer. 2016. Investigating active learning for short-answer scoring. In *Proceedings of BEA-11,* San Diego, California, 16 June 2016, pages 301–311.

Andrea Horbach, Alexis Palmer, and Magdalena Wolska. 2014. Finding a tradeoff between accuracy and rater's workload in grading clustered short answers. In *Proceedings of LREC 2014,* Reykjavik, Iceland, 26–31 May 2014, pages 588–595.

Andrea Horbach and Manfred Pinkal. 2018. Semi-Supervised Clustering for Short Answer Scoring. In *Proceedings of LREC 2018,* Miyazaki, Japan, 7–12 May 2018.

Ludmila I. Kuncheva. 2004. *Combining Pattern Classifiers – Methods and Algorithms.* Wiley, Hoboken, NJ.

Nitin Madnani, Anastassia Loukina, and Aoife Cahill. 2016. A large scale quantitative exploration of modeling strategies for content scoring. In *Proceedings of BEA-12,* Copenhagen, Denmark, 8 September 2017, pages 457–467.

Detmar Meurers, Ramon Ziai, Niels Ott, and Stacey Bailey. 2011a. Integrating parallel analysis modules to evaluate the meaning of answers to reading comprehension questions. *Special Issue on Free-text Automatic Evaluation. International Journal of Continuing Engineering Education and Life-Long Learning (IJCEELL),* 21(4):355–369.

Detmar Meurers, Ramon Ziai, Niels Ott, and Janina Kopp. 2011b. Evaluating answers to reading comprehension questions in context: Results for german and the role of information structure. In *Proceedings of the TextInfer 2011 Workshop on Textual Entailment,* pages 1–9, Edinburgh, Scottland, UK. Association for Computational Linguistics.

Michael Mohler, Razvan Bunescu, and Rada Mihalcea. 2011. Learning to grade short answer questions using semantic similarity measures and dependency graph alignments. In *Proceedings of ACL-HLT 2011,* Portland, Oregon 19–24 June 2011, pages 752–762.

Ulrike Padó. 2016. Get semantic with me! The usefulness of different feature types for short-answer grading. In *Proceedings of COLING 2016,* Osaka, Japan, 13–16 December 2016.

Ulrike Padó. 2017. Question difficulty – How to estimate without norming, how to use for automated grading. In *Proceedings of BEA-12,* Copenhagen, Denmark, 8 September 2017.

Ulrike Padó and Cornelia Kiefer. 2015. Short answer grading: When sorting helps and when it doesn't. In *4th NLP4CALL Workshop at Nodalida,* pages 42–50, Vilnius, Lithuania.

Helen Yannakoudakis and Ronan Cummins. 2015. Evaluating the performance of automated text scoring systems. In *Proceedings of BEA-10,* Denver, Colorado, 4 June 2015, pages 213–223.

Torsten Zesch, Michael Heilmann, and Aoife Cahill. 2015. Reducing annotation efforts in supervised short answer scoring. In *Proceedings of BEA-10,* Denver, Colorado, 4 June 2015, pages 124–132.

Torsten Zesch and Andrea Horbach. 2018. ESCRITO - An NLP-Enhanced Educational Scoring Toolkit. In *Proceedings of LREC 2018,* Miyazaki, Japan, 7–12 May 2018.

NLP Corpus Observatory – Looking for Constellations in Parallel Corpora to Improve Learners' Collocational Skills

Gerold Schneider
English Department &
Institute of Computational Linguistics
University of Zurich
gschneid@ifi.uzh.ch

Johannes Graën
Institute of Computational Linguistics
University of Zurich
graen@cl.uzh.ch

Abstract

The use of corpora in language learning, both in classroom and self-study situations, has proven useful. Investigations into technology use show a benefit for learners that are able to work with corpus data using easily accessible technology. But relatively little work has been done on exploring the possibilities of parallel corpora for language learning applications.

Our work described in this paper explores the applicability of a parallel corpus enhanced with several layers generated by NLP techniques for extracting collocations that are non-compositional and thus indispensable to learn. We identify constellations, i.e. combinations of intra- and interlingual relations, calculate association scores on each relation and, based thereon, a joint score for each constellation. This way, we are able to find relevant collocations for different types of constellations.

We evaluate our approach and discuss scenarios in which language learners can playfully explore collocations. Our explorative web tool is freely accessible, generates collocation dictionaries on the fly, and links them to example sentences to ensure context embedding.

1 Introduction

Parallel corpora show a great potential for language learning, as they allow one to zoom into those areas where the linguistic differences between the native language and the target language are largest.

Data-driven Learning (DDL), although sometimes seen as either too complicated for learners (Hadley and Charles 2017), or furnishing texts of too high levels (Vyatkina and Boulton 2017), can benefit advanced learners, and even beginners, and

also using very basic tools such as concordancers, as e.g. St. John (2001) describes for lexical tasks, Chujo et al. (2016) for grammatical tasks, and Vyatkina (2016) for collocations.

There are ample studies on creating corpus-informed teaching materials, for example dictionaries of collocations (Ackermann and Chen 2013; Durrant 2009; McGee 2012). The advantage of this approach is that students do not need to learn to use corpus interfaces. The disadvantage is that contextualisation is limited. Li (2017) shows that also direct corpus use improves learner competence in the area of collocations. They conclude that "[t]his exposure to attested language data raises learners' awareness of using collocations in a more natural or near-native way …it would be beneficial for more researchers and teachers to investigate direct corpus applications in classroom settings." (p. 165)

Ultimately, we need both corpus-derived teaching material and the direct corpus experience linked to it. Buyse and Verlinde (2013) show that using corpus-derived, contextualised resources (Linguee) led to better test performance and user satisfaction. They suggest that a further integration of tools would be desirable, allowing students to combine the immersion experience which Linguee offers and profit from abstracted customised resources such as collocation dictionaries.

The suggested integration involves using parallel corpora, like Linguee does, but deriving patterns that are particularly challenging for language learners from them, thus creating a registry of lexicogrammmatical phenomena on which learners are likely to experience difficulties because literal translations do not suffice. The desired integration also requires linking the derived patterns back to the test, furnishing contextualised examples. We would like to contribute to this integration with our contribution.

Gerold Schneider and Johannes Graën 2018. NLP Corpus Observatory – Looking for constellations in parallel corpora to improve learners' collocational skills. *Proceedings of the 7th Workshop on NLP for Computer Assisted Language Learning at SLTC 2018 (NLP4CALL 2018)*. Linköping Electronic Conference Proceedings 152: 69–78.

In order not to start with preconceptions, we use as few initial constraints as possible, and let the data point out areas of linguistic contrast. We focus on English compared to Swedish, using four constructions: adjective-noun, verb-preposition, verb-object and verb-preposition-object. Namvar (2012) investigates nine constructions. The results show that verb-object collocations are most frequent in learner writing, followed by verb-preposition collocations. Källkvist (1998) observed that awkward collocations produced by advanced Swedish learners of English often involve an incorrect use of verbs. Verb-preposition constructions are particularly difficult to acquire for language learners (Gilquin and Granger 2011, pp. 59–60). Phrasal verbs represent "one of the most notoriously challenging aspects of English language instruction" (Gardner and Davies 2007, p. 339). Vyatkina (2016) shows particularly good results for learning German verb-particle structures with data-driven learning.

We go beyond purely collocation-based phraseme search, in the following ways: first, while collocations do not entail non-compositionality, the fact that we need to reach collocational status in both languages leads to cleaner results, as in a double check. Secondly, by punishing literal translations, we also filter the majority of instances that are compositional cooccurrences.

In the following, we present a method to explore constellations in parallel corpora. We then present our interactive and explorative web tool, which creates collocation dictionaries on the fly (indirect DDL) based on association scores, and links the dictionary entries to the parallel corpus examples (direct DDL). Users can explore and tailor the association metrics to their needs.

2 Related Work

The bilingual concordancers Glosbe,[1] Linguee,[2] Tradooit[3] and our multilingual Multilingwis[4] (Clematide, Graën, and Volk 2016; Graën and Clematide 2015; Graën, Sandoz, and Volk 2017) are web applications which allow translators and advanced learners to explore and compare translation variants (for an overview, see Volk, Graën,

and Callegaro 2014). No resources such as lists of phrases and collocations for the benefit of learners are automatically derived, however.

There is a long tradition of research in the area of phrasemes (Mel'čuk 1998; Wanner 1996). Collocations measures have been explored systematically (Evert 2004, 2008; Pecina 2009; Church and Hanks 1990) but it is unclear which measures are better suitable for the benefit of language learners.

Huang et al. (2013) present a tool which allows learners to explore collocations using a variety of measures, but the results do not profit from parallel data, e.g. they are not weighted according to translation difficulty, as we intend to do.

To our knowledge, there has been no approach so far where data-driven NLP methods on parallel corpora are used for collocation retrieval for the benefit of language learning. Chujo et al. (2016) is partly similar to our approach. They compare a direct DDL tool in the form of a KWIC concordancer, and a separate indirect tool in the form of a word profiler. The word profiler delivers collocations once the user suggests a node. Our approach is more data-driven, as we assume no given nodes but generate results purely from the parallel corpora, and we fully integrate both into one tool, linking the lists of collocations to the examples in the parallel corpus.

In Graën and Schneider (2017), we describe an approach where word lists are based on parallel corpora, but we restricted our research to the fixed frame of verb-preposition structures, and did not link the lists back to the corpora.

3 Data and Methods

The basis of our experiments is our FEP9 corpus (Graën 2018), which comprises different layers of annotation (part-of-speech tags, lemmas, syntactic dependency relations) and alignment (sentence and word alignment) on top of the cleaned Europarl corpus (Graën, Batinic, and Volk 2014). Europarl (Koehn 2005) consists of the transcribed and translated debates of the European Parliament over a period of 15 years.

From this corpus, we randomly sample a subset of 5% of parallel texts (contributions of individual speakers in Europarl) in English and Swedish. We filter word alignments for those, where three word aligners agree, namely GIZA++ (Och and Ney 2003), the Berkeley Aligner (Liang, Taskar, and Klein 2006) and efmaral (Östling and Tiede-

---

[1]https://glosbe.com
[2]https://www.linguee.com
[3]https://www.tradooit.com
[4]https://pub.cl.uzh.ch/purl/multilingwis

mann 2016). The fourth word aligner available in FEP9, fast_align (Dyer, Chahuneau, and Smith 2013) performs considerably inferior to the other aligners (see Graën 2018, Figure 4.21) and we therefore disregard its alignments. In total, our data set comprises 160 thousand sentence and 2,4 million word alignments.

We count cooccurrence frequencies on syntactic relationships (for each dependency label) and word alignments, both mapped to the respective lemmas in each language. Assuming the independence of two events (i.e. lemmas) observed together in either syntactical (interlingual) or word-correspondence relation (intralingual), we calculate the expected frequency of each lemma pair. Statistical association measures (see Evert 2004, 2008, for an overview) relate the observed frequency (O) to the expected frequency (E) and provide a ranking for a list of cooccurring events. Some association measure yield scores that have an information theoretic interpretation (Evert 2004, Section 3.1.7), but the scores of most measures need to be interpreted in comparison among themselves.

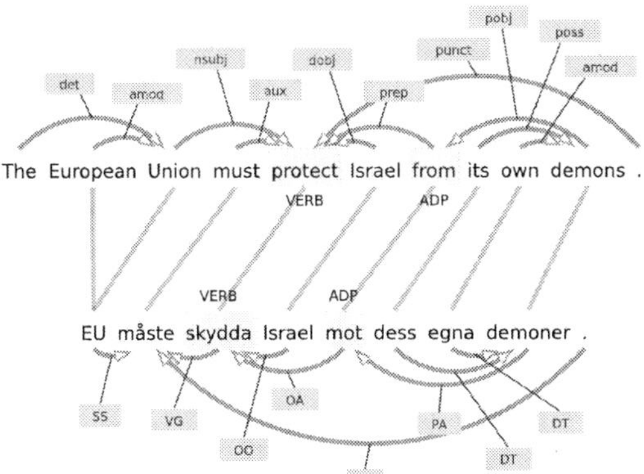

Figure 1: A constellation consisting of two aligned verbs with corresponding aligned prepositions.

Interlingual association measures, that is, the application of well-known association measures, which are frequently used to identify collocations in monolingual corpora, to parallel, word-aligned corpora are first described in (Graën n.d.). Our idea is to combine relations from syntactic analysis with word correspondence (i.e., the output of parsing and word alignment techniques) to find parallel patterns in two languages, which we call constellations. Figure 1 shows an example of parallel verb-preposition structures. Due to their complex structure (syntactic relations in both languages plus word alignment between the two), constellations are more error-prone than monolingual patterns (ibid., Section 4.2). However, the lowest possible threshold of two already suffices to filter out most errors, since systematic errors would need to coincide on the different levels, which is very rare.

We also present an interactive interface that facilitates the exploration of different association measures on different relations (Graën and Bless 2017). Based on a list of verbs and their direct objects, the user chooses one of five "simple association measures" presented in (Evert 2008, Chapter 4) or the absolute frequency for ranking verb-object pairs. On the source language side (English, German or Italian), the association score is either calculated on the syntactic relation between verb and object or one of their alignment relations. This limitation to the original idea of combining association scores on all relations to a single constellation score sketched in (Graën n.d.) is what we address in this work. In addition to support verb constructions with direct objects, we also define constellations for support verb constructions with prepositional objects (see, for instance, Figure 2), adjectival modifiers of noun and verb-preposition combinations.

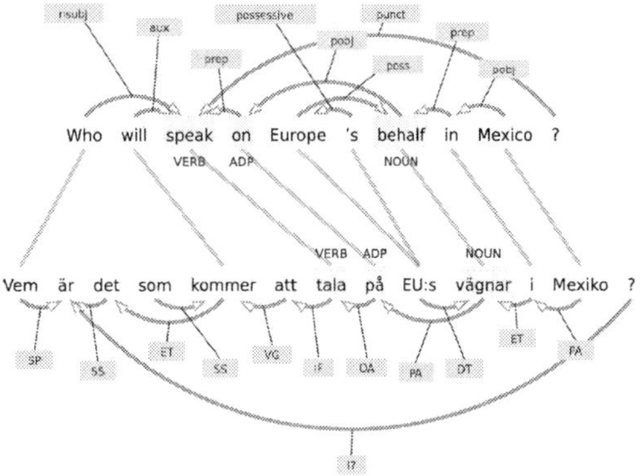

Figure 2: A constellation consisting of two aligned verbs with corresponding aligned prepositions and aligned prepositional objects.

In this work, we implement the idea of free combinations of association scores on different relations. Our objective is to identify non-compositional expressions, such as support verb construction, that a language learner is required to learn by heart. Translation difficulties arise particularly frequently wherever non-compositionality is involved, that is, wherever literal translations lead to incorrect or non-nativelike expressions. Non-compositional features include any form of idiom and collocation, as for example phrasal verbs, support verb constructions and technical terms. We hence combine the parallel search for phrasemes in both languages with word correspondences in the form of alignments.

Retrieval of the constellations from our corpus is similar to the retrieval performed in (Graën n.d.), but we expect that our data holds more reliable word alignments, as they are obtained by agreement of three different word aligners instead of a single one. From the observed (O) and expected (E) cooccurrence frequencies, we calculate the respective association score for each relation. To make different association measures for syntactic dependency relations and word alignment comparable, we normalize all association scores to values between 0 and 1.

A straightforward way to do so is to linearly project all positive association scores to the range from 0 to 1: $score_{norm} = \frac{score}{\max(score)}$. If the maximum association score is attained by an outlier (some association measures favour rare combinations (see Graën 2018, Figure 5.4)), all association scores of the relation in question are penalised.

Another way to normalize values is to use the tangens hyperbolicus: $score_{norm} = 1 - \frac{2}{1+e^{2 \cdot score}}$ Some association measures yield high values that, after being normalized with the tangens hyperbolicus, are indistinguishably close to 1. We therefore propose to apply two subsequent normalisations: first to divide by the average score to obtain a distribution around 1 ($score_{\varnothing} = score/\overline{score}$), and second to apply the tangens hyperbolicus to the resulting normalized scores:

$$score_{norm} = 1 - \frac{2}{1 + e^{score_{\varnothing}}}$$

Our application allows for experimenting with these three normalizations, as well as different association measures for syntactical and word-correspondence relations. The formula for the final score of a particular constellation example can be any mathematical operation on the respective association scores and the raw frequency. As we expect an element of surprise in the correspondence of expressions in both languages, we use the association score on one of the word correspondence relations to downgrade the final score. In the case of support verb constructions, we prefer

verb pairs that are not used frequently as translations. The combinations of association measures that worked best for the respective constellations are explained in Section 4.

We facilitate the memorisation of those expressions by providing authentic parallel corpus examples. The example list comprises all examples from our small corpus subset ordered by number of tokens in both sentences of the respective example (longer sentences are supposed to be more difficult to capture) and the difference in number of tokens between both languages. We expect the latter number to differ since English sentences comprises relatively more tokens than Swedish sentences, but an overly large number typically originates from a non 1-to-1 sentence alignment or untranslated parts in one of the languages. We have considered adding other measures, such as syntactic complexity or variation in alignment, but a length-based sorting already yields satisfactory results. Short sentences allow the user to concentrate on the constellation in context, while long sentences offer so much context that users easily get distracted.

4 Results

Best-scoring results for three different constellations consisting of four tokens are shown on page 7 ff. On page 8, we list the best results for a constellation of six tokens (verbs with prepositional objects). Users can interactively change the collocation formula that are used in our experimental application.

4.1 Adjective-Noun Collocations

For adjective-noun collocations, we show the following formula:

$$score = as_1^2 \cdot as_3^4 \cdot \frac{as_1^3}{(as_2^4)^2}$$

The score consists of the linear combination of the association score between adjective and noun in English (as_1^2) and Swedish (as_3^4), and the association score of the alignment between the nouns (as_3^1), divided by the squared association score of the alignment of the adjectives (as_2^4). This formula has the effect that associations from both languages are reported, particularly those in which the noun is a literal translation, but the adjective is non-literal: the fact that adjective alignment association scores are used in the denominator assures that generally unlikely translations are preferred.

1	When does the Council intend to **reach** a **decision** on the establishment of this future observatory?
	När kommer rådet att **fatta beslut** om att inrätta detta framtida organ?

2	It has attempted to reallocate budgetary resources from the Progress programme to the microfinance facility before the European Parliament has **reached** a **decision**.
	Den har försökt omfördela budgetresurser från Progressprogrammet till instrumentet för mikrokrediter innan Europaparlamentet har **fattat** ett **beslut**.

3	Furthermore, the decision-making process itself can be unclear, as the convention submits proposals and the Intergovernmental Conference has to **reach decisions**.
	Dessutom kan det bli oklart kring själva beslutsfattandet, eftersom konventet lägger fram förslag och regeringskonferensen måste **fatta beslut**.

4	When the matter comes before Parliament, therefore, we often have to **reach** our **decisions** very quickly if we want to make the internal market a reality for the citizens of Europe.
	Kommer ärendet sedan till parlamentet, måste vi ofta **fatta** mycket snabba **beslut**, eftersom vi vill öppna den gemensamma marknaden för medborgarna.

5	With regard to the forestry strategy of the Community in general, and in particular the question whether forestry activities should be governed by Community legislation, the Commission will also shortly **reach** a **decision** on such a forestry strategy, which will likewise be communicated to Parliament.
	Beträffande gemenskapens beskogningsstrategi, i synnerhet frågan om gemenskapsrättsliga bestämmelser för skogsbruket, kommer kommissionen snart att **fatta beslut** om en beskogningsstrategi och informera parlamentet om detta.

6	In **reaching** its **decision** it concluded after prolonged debate, in the presence of Mr Le Pen and colleagues of his who were there to support him, that the legitimate procedure had been complied with in every respect and that no breach of the basic rule establishing parliamentary immunity had taken place, so that the Member was free to carry out his duties while at the same time the institution of Parliament was not being undermined.
	För att **fatta** sitt **beslut** drog det, efter långvarig diskussion där även Le Pen och kolleger som stöder honom var närvarande, slutsatsen att det juridiska förfarandet var absolut korrekt, så att inget brott begås mot grundregeln som fastställer parlamentarisk immunitet, för att ledamoten skall kunna utöva sina plikter oberoende utan att den parlamentariska grundregeln samtidigt undermineras.

Table 1: Examples for the verb-direct object constellation "reach decision"/"fatta beslut" ordered by increasing length and minimal length difference. Example 2 shows a direct translation, sentence 4 shows adjective to adverb variation, sentence 6 an English continuous form.

The 80-best list illustrates that, for example, *stor uppmärksamhet* corresponds to English *great attention*, where the noun is a direct translation, but the adjective is non-literal. Swedish native speakers learning English can thus see that *close attention* is a more native-like translation than *great attention* or even *big attention*. In the opposite direction, English speakers learning Swedish can equally see that *stor uppmärksamhet* is a more native-like translation than *nära uppmärksamhet*.

Clicking on the results displays example sentences sorted by estimated complexity, which helps learners to contextualise idiomatic and collocational expression. We show the example of "reach decision" corresponding to "fatta beslut" (row 4) in Table 1.

4.2 Verb-Object Collocations

For verb-object collocations, we show the following formula:

$$score = as_1^2 \cdot as_3^4 \cdot \frac{as_2^4}{(as_1^3)^2} \cdot freq$$

The formula is similar to the one used for adjective-nouns, this time punishing direct translation of verbs, with the difference that frequency is also used. Frequency is an important factor for the identification of light verb constructions (Ronan and Schneider 2015). Swedish learners of English can see in the table of results that *have de-*

bate is a more native-like translation than *lead debate*, the literal translation, while English learners of Swedish can e.g. see that *nämna exempel* or *ta exempel* is often preferable to the direct translation of *ge exempel*. A further small difference is that we have used the t-score association metric here, while z-score was used for adjective-noun constellations.

The squared association between the verbs has the effect of slightly exaggerating the urge to find verbal differences: the list gives both *have responsibility* as translation of *bära ansvar* (rank 2), as well as *bear responsibility* as translation of *ha ansvar* (rank 175, off the short top of the list). Users can thus experiment with less strong punishment for verb-verb alignment and again inspect the examples, and equally explore a range of association metrics. The interface allows users to interactively and playfully explore native speaker associations.

4.3 Verb-Preposition Collocations

Next, we focus on verb-preposition and phrasal verb constructions. The formula shown here is identical to the one for verb-object, this time punishing direct translations of prepositions (as_2^4 in the denominator is the score calculated on the alignment of the two prepositions):

$$score = as_1^2 \cdot as_3^4 \cdot \frac{as_1^3}{(as_2^4)^2} \cdot freq$$

We can see e.g. that *congratulate on* is a more native-like translation of Swedish *gratulera till* than the direct translation *congratulate to*.

4.4 Verb-Preposition-Object Constellations

Finally, we give an example of a construction involving more than two words: verb-PP constructions where the noun in the PP is also idiomatic.

$$score = as_1^2 \cdot as_2^3 \cdot as_4^5 \cdot as_5^6 \cdot \frac{as_3^6}{(as_1^4)^2} \cdot freq$$

The formula that we illustrate here combines positive association between all the elements except for the verb alignment (as_1^4, where negative association, i.e. non-direct translation is sought for. English learners of Swedish can detect that the idiomatic translation of *come into force* is *träda i kraft*. We also notice that the Swedish lemmatizer is producing a systematic error by lemmatizing the supine form *trätt* to *träta 'to quarrel'* instead of *träda 'to step'*.

5   Evaluation

While the lists presented in Section 4 may look intuitively convincing, the question arises up to which point learners fail to produce the collocations suggested in the lists, and instead produce direct translations, influenced by L1 transfer. We thus address the question if learners actually produce the awkward collocations that the list suggests. As test case, we assume a situation in which a native speaker of Swedish is producing English collocations. The question is whether his or her collocations are less native-like than those in a reference corpus of native speakers. We use the ICLE corpus (Granger et al. 2009) as learner corpus to assess if the level of these awkward collocations is higher in than in a native speaker corpus, for which we use the BNC (Aston and Burnard 1998).

The picture is complicated by several facts. First, the awkward collocations are all correct, and also found in the BNC, but typically with a slight meaning shift, and not as the major variant. We are thus addressing the question if the suggested English collocation is more dominant in the native than in the learner texts. Second, due to sparse data reasons, we had to include all learners, irrespective of their native language. Third, ICLE contains data of University students, advanced learners who chose native-like collocations in the majority of cases.

We evaluate adjective-noun structures, in the two following ways. First, for all cases where

- the Swedish adjective has a direct translation,

- one that is different from the one suggested in the collocation under observation,

- but semantically similar to the English one in the list,

- the translation of the noun is direct,

- whenever we have at least 3 hits in ICLE in total (maximally one zero count in any cell is replaced by a smoothing count of 0.1)

then we compare the numbers.

For example, *stor uppmärksomhet* (t_4, t_3) could be directly translated to English *great attention* (t_2', t_1), but the suggested English collocation is *close attention* (t_2, t_1). *close attention* occurs 106 times in the BNC, *great attention* only 47 times, the ratio $r_{\text{BNC}} = t_2/t_2'$ is 2.25. In ICLE, *great attention* occurs 9 times, while *close attention* occurs twice,

Adjective-Noun Constellations (4.1)

no.	t_2 (adj. en)	t_1 (noun en)	t_4 (adj. sv)	t_3 (noun sv)	freq.	as_1^2	as_3^4	as_1^3	as_2^4	score
1	close	attention	stor	uppmärksamhet	2	0.0530	0.0669	0.7312	0.0009	2959.5
2	more	time	lång	tid	2	0.0274	0.2662	0.4821	0.0023	635.9
3	top	priority	viktig	prioritering	2	0.2380	0.0493	0.6815	0.0041	481.0
4	large	number	lång	rad	2	0.2108	0.2087	0.1585	0.0057	213.3
5	monetary	policy	ekonomisk	politik	3	0.0939	0.1192	0.6253	0.0066	161.9
6	young	child	liten	barn	3	0.0460	0.0746	0.9397	0.0047	145.2
7	valuable	contribution	viktig	bidrag	2	0.1160	0.0805	0.6603	0.0066	141.2
8	whole	series	lång	rad	2	0.1546	0.2087	0.4516	0.0102	139.2
9	regulatory	framework	rättslig	ram	2	0.1168	0.1266	0.5619	0.0079	131.9
10	constructive	cooperation	god	samarbete	2	0.0470	0.0445	0.8323	0.0041	101.4
11	important	role	stor	roll	2	0.0933	0.0211	0.8691	0.0044	90.3
12	lead	committee	ansvarig	utskott	2	0.0236	0.1680	0.4987	0.0052	73.6
13	fellow	member	kär	kollega	2	0.2643	0.6567	0.1196	0.0182	62.8
14	absolute	priority	hög	prioritet	2	0.0737	0.1601	0.3575	0.0088	53.9
15	central	question	viktig	fråga	2	0.0149	0.1409	0.5068	0.0047	49.0
16	whole	range	lång	rad	2	0.1421	0.2087	0.1575	0.0102	44.6
17	last	year	gången	år	5	0.2675	0.2123	0.9221	0.0346	43.7
18	particular	case	konkret	fall	3	0.0583	0.0557	0.7535	0.0076	42.6
19	excellent	report	bra	betänkande	5	0.2209	0.0643	0.8447	0.0181	36.6
20	good	deal	hel	del	3	0.0266	0.2168	0.0371	0.0024	36.3
21	paramount	importance	stor	vikt	2	0.1651	0.1405	0.4416	0.0178	32.3
22	recent	year	gången	år	2	0.1575	0.2123	0.9221	0.0313	31.5
23	much	time	lång	tid	3	0.0306	0.2662	0.4821	0.0120	27.4
24	positive	result	god	resultat	2	0.0654	0.0616	0.6390	0.0102	24.9
25	less	time	kort	tid	2	0.0167	0.1730	0.4821	0.0078	22.7

Verb-Object Constellations (4.2)

no.	t_1 (verb en)	t_2 (noun en)	t_3 (verb sv)	t_4 (noun sv)	freq.	as_1^2	as_3^4	as_1^3	as_2^4	score
1	have	question	ställa	fråga	4	0.9346	0.9977	0.0609	0.8862	891.11
2	have	responsibility	bära	ansvar	2	0.9846	0.9493	0.0393	0.7342	889.74
3	have	debate	föra	debatt	6	0.9554	0.9152	0.0892	0.8882	586.13
4	reach	decision	fatta	beslut	6	0.8145	0.9996	0.0859	0.8266	546.78
5	raise	issue	diskutera	fråga	3	0.9598	0.9759	0.0682	0.9054	546.62
6	make	decision	fatta	beslut	43	0.9779	0.9996	0.2533	0.8266	541.74
7	take	decision	fatta	beslut	58	0.9908	0.9996	0.3194	0.8266	465.47
8	achieve	solution	finna	lösning	2	0.6987	0.9835	0.0478	0.7343	441.00
9	assume	responsibility	ta	ansvar	16	0.9139	0.9958	0.1564	0.7342	437.24
10	play	role	ha	roll	5	0.9991	0.9856	0.0942	0.7497	416.01
11	draw	attention	fästa	uppmärksamhet	34	0.9982	0.9694	0.2090	0.5319	400.66
12	give	example	nämna	exempel	3	0.9057	0.7921	0.0637	0.7493	397.32
13	adopt	decision	fatta	beslut	4	0.7181	0.9996	0.0778	0.8266	392.14
14	solve	problem	lösa	problem	63	0.9946	0.9985	0.3853	0.9118	384.33
15	shoulder	responsibility	ta	ansvar	6	0.6800	0.9958	0.0931	0.7342	344.14
16	pave	way	bana	väg	18	0.9175	0.9215	0.1489	0.4915	337.31
17	accept	responsibility	ta	ansvar	15	0.8333	0.9958	0.1648	0.7342	336.37
18	draw	attention	rikta	uppmärksamhet	15	0.9982	0.9000	0.1487	0.5319	323.94
19	fulfil	responsibility	ta	ansvar	2	0.5265	0.9958	0.0488	0.7342	322.95
20	adopt	measure	vidta	åtgärd	18	0.9296	0.9999	0.2109	0.8489	319.34
21	assume	responsibility	axla	ansvar	3	0.9139	0.5926	0.0612	0.7342	318.83
22	play	role	spela	roll	120	0.9991	0.9997	0.5311	0.7497	318.59
23	take	place	äga	rum	155	1.0000	0.9993	0.5510	0.6058	309.03
24	give	example	ta	exempel	3	0.9057	0.7758	0.0715	0.7493	308.60
25	ask	question	ställa	fråga	36	0.9671	0.9977	0.3421	0.8862	262.96

Verb-Preposition Constellations (4.3)

no.	t_1 (verb en)	t_2 (prep. en)	t_3 (verb sv)	t_4 (prep. sv)	freq.	as_1^2	as_3^4	as_1^3	as_2^4	score
1	deal	with	handla	om	5	0.3824	0.4725	0.0406	6.5E-7	8.6E10
2	cover	by	falla	under	2	0.1300	0.1232	0.0125	0.0001	63633.7
3	congratulate	on	gratulera	till	64	0.2754	0.1862	0.8401	0.0238	4868.7
4	play	in	spela	för	3	0.0979	0.0606	0.8301	0.0018	4818.8
5	agree	with	instämma	i	13	0.4470	0.1311	0.3070	0.0073	4429.4
6	work	on	arbeta	med	39	0.1970	0.1676	0.4541	0.0188	1648.3
7	protect	from	skydda	mot	12	0.0825	0.1479	0.7639	0.0107	975.8
8	base	on	utgå	från	8	0.3929	0.2969	0.0760	0.0087	932.1
9	aim	at	sträva	efter	3	0.3673	0.7869	0.0693	0.0089	762.1
10	vary	from	variera	mellan	4	0.0701	0.1292	0.6337	0.0057	705.1
11	engage	in	ägna	åt	3	0.0871	0.8751	0.0609	0.0045	680.5
12	bring	about	leda	till	7	0.1376	0.3622	0.0442	0.0051	598.7
13	ask	for	be	om	27	0.2278	0.1337	0.5357	0.0306	470.0
14	wait	for	vänta	på	6	0.1821	0.1407	0.6473	0.0169	349.4
15	be	with	vara	i	2	0.0368	0.3080	0.7931	0.0073	340.2
16	work	towards	arbeta	för	15	0.2052	0.1058	0.4541	0.0217	314.2
17	be	in	vara	mot	2	0.2576	0.0608	0.7931	0.0090	308.3
18	be	from	vara	i	2	0.0382	0.3176	0.7931	0.0079	305.7
19	spend	on	ägna	åt	2	0.0701	0.8751	0.1198	0.0071	292.4
20	talk	about	tala	om	150	1.0000	0.3575	0.4997	0.3041	289.8
21	think	about	tänka	på	3	0.1357	0.2119	0.1836	0.0084	223.1
22	be	for	vara	av	12	0.1366	0.2122	0.7931	0.0389	182.4
23	be	at	vara	i	11	0.3520	0.3704	0.7931	0.0819	169.4
24	begin	by	börja	med	54	0.1891	0.2438	0.4637	0.0841	163.3
25	think	of	tänka	på	7	0.0594	0.2115	0.1836	0.0104	149.0

Verb-Preposition-Noun Constellations (4.4)

no.	t_1 (verb en)	t_2 (prep)	t_3 (noun)	t_4 (verb sv)	t_5 (prep)	t_6 (noun)	freq.	as_1^4	as_2^5	as_3^6	score
1	vote	for	report	rösta	för	betänkande	54	1.0000	1.0000	1.0000	54.000
2	enter	into	force	träda	i	kraft	31	0.9958	1.0000	1.0000	31.258
3	thank	for	work	tacka	för	arbete	31	1.0000	1.0000	1.0000	31.000
4	be	in	interest	ligga	i	intresse	29	1.0000	1.0000	1.0000	28.999
5	thank	for	report	tacka	för	betänkande	25	1.0000	1.0000	1.0000	25.000
6	be	of	importance	vara	av	betydelse	25	1.0000	1.0000	1.0000	25.000
7	congratulate	on	report	gratulera	till	betänkande	18	1.0000	1.0000	1.0000	18.000
8	vote	against	report	rösta	mot	betänkande	18	1.0000	1.0000	1.0000	17.971
9	speak	with	voice	tala	med	röst	18	1.0000	1.0000	0.9998	17.825
10	come	from	country	komma	från	land	16	1.0000	1.0000	1.0000	16.000
11	vote	for	resolution	rösta	för	resolution	16	1.0000	1.0000	1.0000	15.987
12	thank	for	cooperation	tacka	för	samarbete	15	1.0000	1.0000	1.0000	15.000
13	be	of	importance	vara	av	vikt	15	1.0000	1.0000	1.0000	15.000
14	be	at	stake	stå	på	spel	13	1.0000	1.0000	0.9866	12.824
15	come	into	force	träda	i	kraft	12	0.9865	1.0000	1.0000	12.329
16	participate	in	debate	delta	i	debatt	12	1.0000	1.0000	1.0000	12.000
17	take	on	Thursday	äga	på	torsdag	12	1.0000	1.0000	0.9996	11.856
18	go	in	hand	gå	i	hand	11	1.0000	1.0000	0.9999	10.999
19	thank	for	support	tacka	för	stöd	11	1.0000	1.0000	1.0000	10.997
20	enter	into	force	träta	i	kraft	9	0.9300	1.0000	1.0000	10.280
21	propose	by	Commission	föreslå	av	kommission	10	1.0000	1.0000	1.0000	9.971
22	be	in	situation	befinna	i	situation	9	1.0000	1.0000	1.0000	9.001
23	adopt	by	Committee	anta	av	utskott	9	1.0000	1.0000	1.0000	8.997
24	contribute	to	development	bidra	till	utveckling	9	1.0000	1.0000	1.0000	8.996
25	be	in	line	ligga	i	linje	9	1.0000	1.0000	0.9998	8.995

no.	t_2, t_1	t_4, t_3	BNC Hits	BNC total	ICLE Hits	ICLE total	dominance BNC/ICLE	direct Translation of t_4	BNC direct	ICLE direct	ratio r
1	close, attention	stor, uppmärksamhet	106	4805	2	286	3.15	great	47	9	10.15
5	monetary, policy	ekonomisk, politik	566	24294	5	420	1.96	economic	1050	12	1.29
6	young, child	liten, barn	1380	19452	75	1427	1.35	small	182	63	6.37
7	valuable, contribution	viktig, bidrag	89	4702	1	88	1.67	important	208	4	1.71
9	regulatory, framework	rättslig, ram	56	3053	0.1	22	4.04	legal	160	1	3.50
11	important, role	stor, roll	723	11027	257	763	0.19	big	12	22	5.16
14	absolute, priority	hög, prioritet	18	2239	1	45	0.36	high	220	1	0.08
15	central, question	viktig, fråga	90	12703	0.1	669	47.40	important	317	51	144.79
24	positive, result	god, resultat	268	10533	12	435	0.92	good	268	28	2.33
30	important, progress	stor, framsteg	10	2870	3	363	0.42	big	0.1	3	100.00
32	substantial, progress	viktig, framsteg	56	2870	1	363	7.08	important	10	0.1	0.56
34	serious, problem	stor, problem	594	24420	318	3470	0.27	big	175	109	1.16
38	good, opportunity	stor, möjlighet	119	5984	25	732	0.58	big	11	2	0.87
∅							5.34				21.38

Table 2: Evaluation of adjective-noun constellations

$r_{\text{ICLE}} = t_2/t_2'$ is 0.22. r_{BNC} divided by r_{ICLE} (r, last column) is then 10.15, which can be interpreted as relative dominance, expressing that the suggested collocation is 10.15 times more dominant in the BNC than in ICLE. We can see in Table 2 that the mean of this dominance is about 21. There are cases where the suggested English collocation rarer in BNC, though: *absolute priority* and *substantial progress* is more narrow and specific than the direct translations, *high priority* and *important progress*.

Second, we measure the absolute dominance of the English collocation, as follows: the frequency of the collocation, divided by the frequency of the noun modified by any adjective. For *close attention* in the BNC, this is $dom(\text{BNC}) = 106/4805 = 0.022$, in ICLE it is $dom(\text{ICLE}) = 2/286 = 0.007$. $dom(\text{BNC})/dom(\text{ICLE})$ is thus 3.15. The mean of the absolute dominance is 5.3, which means that the suggested collocation is found 5.3 times more often in BNC than in ICLE.

The evaluation has shown that in the majority of cases, our method yields good results, and allows learners to explore various constellations.

6 Conclusions and Future Work

We have implemented and evaluated an interactive tool for data-driven learning of constellations (i.e., parallel collocation structures) in which language learners experience particular difficulties.[5] Our system features full integration of direct and indirect data-driven learning. Collocation dictionaries are generated on the fly, and linked to the parallel examples in the aligned corpus to ensure contextualisation. Our approach is based on the use of association measures of collocations and of alignments. Advanced users can also customise the association scores.

As future steps, we plan to test the tool with learners, to train on the entire Europarl corpus, and to add more languages to our approach.

---

[5] https://pub.cl.uzh.ch/purl/constellations

References

Ackermann, K. and Y. H. Chen (2013). "Developing the Academic Collocation List (ACL): A corpus- driven and expert-judged approach." In: *Journal of English for Academic Purposes* I2.4, pp. 235–247.

Aston, G. and L. Burnard (1998). *The BNC Handbook. Exploring the British National Corpus with SARA*. Edinburgh: Edinburgh University Press.

Buyse, K. and S. Verlinde (2013). "Possible effects of free on line data driven lexicographic instruments on foreign language learning: The case of Linguee and the interactive language toolbox". In: *Procedia-Social and Behavioral Sciences* 95, pp. 507–512.

Chujo, K., Y. Kobayashi, A. Mizumoto, and K. Oghigian (2016). "Exploring the Effectiveness of Combined Web-based Corpus Tools for Beginner". In: *Linguistics and Literature Studies* 4.4, pp. 262–274.

Church, K. W. and P. Hanks (1990). "Word Association Norms, Mutual Information, and Lexicography". In: *Computational Linguistics* 16.1, pp. 22–29.

Clematide, S., J. Graën, and M. Volk (2016). "Multilingwis – A Multilingual Search Tool for Multi-Word Units in Multiparallel Corpora". In: *Computerised and Corpus-based Approaches to Phraseology: Monolingual and Multilingual Perspectives – Fraseologia computacional y basada en corpus: perspectivas monolingües y multilingües*. Ed. by G. C. Pastor. Geneva: Tradulex, pp. 447–455.

Durrant, P. (2009). "Investigating the viability of a collocation list for students of English for academic purposes". In: *English for Specific Purposes* 28.3, pp. 157–169.

Dyer, C., V. Chahuneau, and N. A. Smith (2013). "A Simple, Fast, and Effective Reparameterization of IBM Model 2". In: *Proceedings of the Conference of the North American Chapter of the Association for Computational Linguistics: Human Language Technologies (NAACL-HLT)*. Association for Computational Linguistics (ACL), pp. 644–649.

Evert, S. (2004). "The Statistics of Word Cooccurrences: Word Pairs and Collocations". PhD thesis. University of Stuttgart.

– (2008). "Corpora and collocations". In: *Corpus Linguistics. An International Handbook*. Ed. by A. Lüdeling and M. Kytö. Vol. 2. Berlin: Walter de Gruyter, pp. 1212–1248.

Gardner, D. and M. Davies (2007). "Pointing out frequent phrasal verbs: A corpus-based analysis". In: *TESOL Quarterly: A Journal for Teachers of English to Speakers of Other Languages and of Standard English as a Second Dialect* 41.2, pp. 339–359.

Gilquin, G. and S. Granger (2011). "From EFL to ESL: Evidence from the International Corpus of Learner English". In: *Exploring Second-Language Varieties of English and Learner Englishes: Bridging a Paradigm Gap*. Ed. by J. Mukherjee and M. Hundt. Amsterdam: John Benjamins, pp. 55–78.

Graën, J. (n.d.). "Identifying Phrasemes via Interlingual Association Measures". In: *Lexemkombinationen und typisierte Rede im mehrsprachigen Kontext*. Ed. by C. Konecny, E. Autelli, A. Abel, and L. Zanasi. Tübingen: Stauffenburg Linguistik. In press.

– (2018). "Exploiting Alignment in Multiparallel Corpora for Applications in Linguistics and Language Learning". PhD thesis. University of Zurich. In press.

Graën, J., D. Batinic, and M. Volk (Oct. 2014). "Cleaning the Europarl Corpus for Linguistic Applications". In: *Proceedings of the Conference on Natural Language Processing (KONVENS)* (Hildesheim). Stiftung Universität Hildesheim, pp. 222–227.

Graën, J. and C. Bless (2017). "Exploring Properties of Intralingual and Interlingual Association Measures Visually". In: *Proceedings of the 21st Nordic Conference of Computational Linguistics (NODALIDA)*. Linköping Electronic Conference Proceedings 131. Linköping University Electronic Press, Linköpings universitet, pp. 314–317.

Graën, J. and S. Clematide (2015). "Challenges in the Alignment, Management and Exploitation of Large and Richly Annotated Multi-Parallel Corpora". In: *Proceedings of the 3rd Workshop on Challenges in the Management of Large Corpora (CMLC)* (Lancaster). Ed. by P. Bański, H. Biber, et al., pp. 15–20.

Graën, J., D. Sandoz, and M. Volk (2017). "Multilingwis² – Explore Your Parallel Corpus". In: *Proceedings of the 21st Nordic Conference of Computational Linguistics (NODALIDA)*. Linköping Electronic Conference Proceedings 131. Linköping University Electronic Press, Linköpings universitet, pp. 247–250.

Graën, J. and G. Schneider (2017). "Crossing the Border Twice: Reimporting Prepositions to Alleviate L1-Specific Transfer Errors". In: *Proceedings of the Joint 6th Workshop on NLP for Computer Assisted Language Learning & 2nd Workshop on NLP for Research on Language Acquisition*. Linköping Electronic Conference Proceedings 134. Linköpings universitet Electronic Press, pp. 18–26.

Granger, S., E. Dagneaux, F. Meunier, and M. Paquot (2009). *International Corpus of Learner English v2 (Handbook + CD-Rom)*. Presses universitaires de Louvain. Louvain-la-Neuve.

Hadley, G. and M. Charles (2017). "Enhancing extensive reading with data-driven learning". In: *Language Learning & Technology* 21.3, pp. 131–152.

Huang, P.-Y., C.-M. Chen, N.-L. Tsao, and D. Wible (2013). "A Corpus-Based Tool for Exploring Domain-Specific Collocations in English". In: *27th Pacific Asia Conference on Language, Information, and Computation (PACLIC)*, pp. 542–549.

Källkvist, M. (1998). "Lexical infelicity in English: the case of nouns and verbs". English. In: *Perspectives on Lexical Acquisition in a Second Language*. Ed. by K. Haastrup and Å. Viberg. Lund University Press.

Koehn, P. (2005). "Europarl: A parallel corpus for statistical machine translation". In: *Machine Translation Summit* (Phuket). Vol. 5. Asia-Pacific Association for Machine Translation, pp. 79–86.

Li, S. (2017). "Using corpora to develop learners' collocational competence". In: *Language Learning & Technology* 21.3, pp. 153–171.

Liang, P., B. Taskar, and D. Klein (2006). "Alignment by Agreement". In: *Proceedings of the Conference of the North American Chapter of the Association for Computational Linguistics: Human Language Technologies (NAACL-HLT)*. Association for Computational Linguistics (ACL), pp. 104–111.

McGee, I. (2012). "Collocation dictionaries as inductive learning resources in data-driven learning: An analysis and evaluation". In: *International Journal of Lexicography* 25.3, pp. 319–361.

Mel'čuk, I. (1998). "Collocations and Lexical Functions". In: *Phraseology. Theory, Analysis, and Applications*. Ed. by A. P. Cowie, pp. 23–53.

Namvar, F. (Jan. 2012). "The relationship between language proficiency and use of collocation by Iranian EFL students". In: *The Southeast Asian Journal of English Language Studies* 18 (3), pp. 41–52.

Och, F. J. and H. Ney (2003). "A Systematic Comparison of Various Statistical Alignment Models". In: *Computational Linguistics* 29.1, pp. 19–51.

Östling, R. and J. Tiedemann (2016). "Efficient word alignment with Markov Chain Monte Carlo". In: *Prague Bulletin of Mathematical Linguistics* 106, pp. 125–146.

Pecina, P. (2009). *Lexical Association Measures: Collocation Extraction*. Vol. 4. Studies in Computational and Theoretical Linguistics. Praha, Czech Republic: Institute of Formal and Applied Linguistics, Charles University in Prague.

Ronan, P. and G. Schneider (2015). "Determining Light Verb Constructions in Contemporary British and Irish English". In: *International Journal of Corpus Linguistics* 20.3, pp. 326–354.

St. John, E. (2001). "A case for using a parallel corpus and concordancer for beginners of a foreign language". In: *Language Learning & Technology* 5.3, pp. 185–203.

Volk, M., J. Graën, and E. Callegaro (2014). "Innovations in Parallel Corpus Search Tools". In: *Proceedings of the 9th International Conference on Language Resources and Evaluation (LREC)* (Reykjavik). Ed. by N. Calzolari et al. European Language Resources Association (ELRA), pp. 3172–3178.

Vyatkina, N. (2016). "Data-driven learning for beginners: The case of German verb-preposition collocations Data-driven learning for beginners: The case of German verb-preposition collocations". In: *ReCALL* 28.2, pp. 207–226.

Vyatkina, N. and A. Boulton (2017). "Corpora in language learning and teaching: Commentary". In: *Language Learning & Technology* 21.3, pp. 1–8.

Wanner, L. (1996). *Lexical Functions in Lexicography and Natural Language Processing*. Vol. 31. John Benjamins Publishing.

A Linguistically-Informed Search Engine to Identifiy Reading Material for Functional Illiteracy Classes

Zarah Weiss   **Sabrina Dittrich**   **Detmar Meurers**
Department of Linguistics, ICALL-Research.de Group
LEAD Graduate School & Research Network
University of Tübingen
{zweiss,dm}@sfs.uni-tuebingen.de,
sabrina.dittrich@uni-tuebingen.de

Abstract

We present KANSAS, a search engine designed to retrieve reading materials for functional illiterates and learners of German as a Second Language. The system allows teachers to refine their searches for teaching material by selecting appropriate readability levels and (de)prioritizing linguistic constructions. In addition to this linguistically-informed query result ranking, the system provides visual input enhancement for the selected linguistic constructions.

Our system combines state-of-the-art Natural Language Processing (NLP) with light-weight algorithms for the identification of relevant linguistic constructions. We have evaluated the system in two pilot studies in terms of the identification of linguistic constructions and the identification of readability levels. Both pilots achieved highly promising results and are being followed by full-fledged performance studies and usability tests.

1   Introduction

We present KANSAS, a linguistically-informed search engine designed to support teachers for adult literacy and German as a Second Language (GSL) classes in their search for appropriate reading materials.[1] Functional illiteracy describes the inability to read or write short coherent texts. This includes the inability to comprehend everyday reading materials such as information brochures or operating instructions. It is a pressing issue for modern society; approximately 7.5 million people in Germany are functional illiterates, which corresponds to 14.5% of the working-age population (18-64 years) (Riekmann and Grotlüschen,

2011). For teachers of adult literacy classes, it is particularly difficult to find reading material that is appropriate for their students. While the need for authentic reading material with particular linguistic characteristics has also been pointed out for foreign language teaching (Chinkina et al., 2016), the issue in the functional illiteracy context is even more pressing given that adult literacy classrooms are highly culturally and linguistically diverse. Learners have heterogeneous biographical and educational backgrounds, they may or may not be native speakers of German, and their low literacy skills may or may not be associated with a cognitive disability, which is commonly considered to include, among others, populations with Autism Spectrum Disorders (ASD), dyslexia, intellectual disorders, traumatic brain injuries, aphasia, dementia, Alzheimer's disease, and Attention Deficit (Hyperactivity) Disorder (Friedman and Bryen, 2007; Huenerfauth et al., 2009). This substantial diversity has to be considered when selecting teaching materials, also making the use of textbooks particularly questionable. In practice, adult literacy teachers depend on identifying appropriate materials for their classes online using standard content search engines like *Google* or *Bing*. However, identifying adequate reading material for readers with lower reading skills is a challenging task: Huenerfauth et al. (2009) and Feng (2009) point out that many texts that are accessible at low literacy levels actually target children and their content may thus be ill-suited for adult readers; texts of interest to adult readers often require higher levels of literacy. Vajjala and Meurers (2013) show that the reading level of web query results obtained using *Bing* is variable, but on average quite high. Web content specifically designed for readers with low reading skills is not necessarily suited for all learners either, due to the diversity of conditions that result in low literacy

---

[1] https://www.kansas-suche.de/

Zarah Weiss, Sabrina Dittrich and Detmar Meurers 2018. A linguistically-informed search engine to identifiy reading material for functional illiteracy classes. *Proceedings of the 7th Workshop on NLP for Computer Assisted Language Learning at SLTC 2018 (NLP4CALL 2018)*. Linköping Electronic Conference Proceedings 152: 79–90.

skills (Yaneva, 2015). Our system is designed to support teachers in this challenging task of identifying appropriate material by combining content queries with the flexible (de)prioritization of relevant linguistic constructions and filtering results by readability levels.

The system design is based on insights from Second Language Acquisition (SLA) research. Similar to SLA, the acquisition of reading and writing skills, even in the L1, does not happen implicitly through exposure but through explicit instruction. Thus, insights from SLA research are highly relevant for the context of literacy training. The importance of *input* for successful language acquisition is well-established in SLA research (Krashen, 1977; Swain, 1985). According to Krashen's *Input Hypothesis* (Krashen, 1977), learning is facilitated by exposure to input that is slightly more advanced than a learner's current state of language competence (*i+1*). We promote the identification of appropriate texts by offering a readability level filter that is designed to specifically target the reading competence of functional illiterates. Another insight from SLA research that we included in the design of our system is that the salience of linguistic constructions and the recognition of these constructions by the learner is a crucial component of language learning, as established by Schmidt's *Noticing Hypothesis* (Schmidt, 1990). One prominent approach to promote salience of linguistic constructions is (visual) *input enhancement* (Smith, 1993) in terms of, e.g., colors, font changes, or spacing. KANSAS integrates these two aspects by i) giving users the option to promote search results that contain relevant linguistic constructions and by ii) visually enhancing these constructions in the reading text. By taking the perspective of SLA research into consideration, we also approach a broader group of learners, including GSL. This matches the reality of most German literacy classes, which are not only attended by native speakers with reading deficiencies but also by some non-native speakers. Also, while KANSAS is designed for educational purposes and focuses on the functional illiterate reading population, it can also facilitate the identification of well-suited reading materials in ordinary web searches conducted by users with low literacy skills, who face the same issues as literacy teachers when it comes to the identification of accessible reading materi-als (Eraslan et al., 2017; McCarthy and Swierenga, 2010).

The article is structured as follows: First, we give some background on related work. In Section 3, we then describe our system's technical implementation and general workflow. We put a special focus on its two main components: the algorithm for the identification of relevant linguistic constructions and the readability assessment algorithm. We then present the preliminary evaluation of these two algorithms from two pilot studies, which are currently being extended by follow up studies. We conclude with an outlook on future steps.

2   Background

In addition to other information retrieval systems that have been designed for the purpose of language acquisition, our work heavily draws on previous work on readability assessment in the context of SLA research, research on the accessibility of reading materials for users with cognitive disabilities, and specifically on German illiteracy research.

2.1   Related Systems

The idea of retrieving and making use of authentic web texts for language learning purposes has been investigated in several research approaches.

The ICALL systems *VIEW* and *WERTi* provide input enhancement techniques for websites (Meurers et al., 2010). They support visually enhancing selected linguistic constructions in order to make them more salient to the learner. Furthermore, they automatically generate fill-in-the-gap exercises for these constructions and embed them into the websites in real-time.

Another productive line of research investigates the design of search engines for language learners. The *REAP* tutoring system (Brown and Eskenazi, 2004) helps selecting appropriate reading material from a digital library data base by matching texts against a student model focusing on vocabulary acquisition. It has also been ported to Portuguese (Marujo et al., 2009). Ott and Meurers (2011) developed *LAWSE*, a search engine prototype that takes reading difficulty measures into account. A similar system is READ-X (Miltsakaki and Troutt, 2007), a search engine that analyzes text readability by making use of traditional readability formula.

Finally, the *FLAIR* system (Form-Focused Linguistically Aware Information Retrieval) by Chinkina et al. (2016) emphasizes the importance of including grammar knowledge into such information retrieval systems. *FLAIR* integrates grammatical patterns specified in an official English L2 class curriculum into a content-based search engine. The system allows users to rerank search results by assigning weights to linguistic constructions. Furthermore, it visually enhances these constructions in a simple reading view and allows to filter texts for readability based on a readability formula. KANSAS adapts *FLAIR* to German and focuses primarily on the special needs of functional literacy training.

2.2 Readability Assessment

Readability assessment is the task of matching texts to readers of a certain population based on the (linguistic) complexity of the text. The earliest approach is the use of simple readability formulas such as the Flesch-Kincaid formula (Kincaid et al., 1975) or the Dale-Chall readability formula (Chall and Dale, 1995); see DuBay (2006) for an overview. These formulas are still widely used in non-linguistic studies (Esfahani et al., 2016; Grootens-Wiegers et al., 2015) and in information retrieval systems (cf. Section 2.1). However, readability formulas are known to be highly limited and potentially unreliable as they only capture superficial text properties such as sentence and word length (Feng et al., 2009; Benjamin, 2012). Research on readability assessment thus has shifted towards broader linguistic modeling of syntactic, lexical, and discourse complexity based on elaborate Natural Language Processing (NLP) pipelines and successfully adopted features from SLA research (Feng et al., 2010; Vajjala and Meurers, 2012). Measures of discourse and textual cohesion were also shown to be highly relevant for readability assessment (Crossley et al., 2008, 2011; Feng et al., 2009), as well as psycho-linguistic measures of language use (Chen and Meurers, 2017; Weiss and Meurers, 2018). While most work on readability assessment was conducted for English, the findings have also been corroborated for other languages such as French (François and Fairon, 2012), Italian (Dell'Orletta et al., 2011), and German (Vor der Brück et al., 2008; Hancke et al., 2012; Weiss and Meurers, 2018).

These data-driven machine learning approaches

to readability modeling are not feasible for these populations due to a lack of (labeled) training data (Yaneva et al., 2016). Although there are corpus-based approaches to comparative readability assessment for low literacy readers (cf., e.g., Feng et al., 2009; Yaneva et al., 2016), eye-tracking studies are more common in research on readability assessment for these groups: Rello et al. investigate the effect of noun frequency and noun length (Rello et al., 2013a) and the effect of number representations (Rello et al., 2013b) on the readability and comprehensibility of texts for Spanish L1 readers with dyslexia. Eraslan et al. (2017) investigate general information extraction strategies of users with high functioning autism on web pages using eye-tracking and Yaneva et al. (2015) employ eye-tracking to study attention patterns of readers with ASD in contextualized documents containing images as well as text material. They derive recommendations from their findings to improve text accessibility for readers with low literacy skills. Among other things, they recommend the use of plain English matching Easy-to-Read requirements as suitable in their complexity for readers with ASD. With this, they link eye-tracking research to another increasingly popular approach for the evaluation of reading materials for populations with cognitive disabilities: the adherence to guidelines for the production of Easy-to-Read materials. Easy-to-Read materials are specifically designed to enhance the accessibility of texts for readers with cognitive disabilities; examples are the guidelines by Nomura et al. (2010) and Freyhoff et al. (1998). These guidelines comment on text layout as well as on language complexity. Yaneva (2015) operationalizes some of the language-focused recommendations in Freyhoff et al. (1998)'s Easy-to-Read guidelines in terms of automatically accessible linguistic features. She uses the resulting algorithm to evaluate web material marked as Easy-to-Read document in terms of their compliance to these guidelines and their similarity to material specifically designed for two target populations of Easy-to-Read language: readers with ASD and readers with mild ID. Yaneva et al. (2016) use this algorithm to evaluate reading materials for readers with cognitive disabilities in terms of their compliance to Easy-to-Read standards.

2.3 Functional Illiteracy

Two major studies have addressed the issue of functional illiteracy in Germany: The *lea. - Literalitätsentwicklung von Arbeitskräften* study ("literacy development for workers") and the *leo. - Level-One* study.[2] They defined degrees of (functional) illiteracy and severely low reading and writing abilities. They define functional illiteracy as reading and writing skills at which individual sentences may be written or read, but not coherent texts even if they are short. Severely low reading and writing abilities are above the level of functional illiteracy, but at this level literacy competence is still highly limited and does not exceed short or intermediate texts. In the course of these studies, the so called *Alpha Levels* were developed to systematically address degrees of limited literacy in the German population (Riekmann and Grotlüschen, 2011). Alpha levels range from Alpha 1 to Alpha 6. Reading and writing skills at Alpha Levels 1 to 3 constitute functional illiteracy, while Alpha Levels 4 to 6 describe varying degrees of low literacy. Table 1 displays the reading skill dimension of these levels.

We used these descriptions of reading and writing competencies across Alpha Levels to derive corresponding criteria reading materials have to adhere to in order to be suitable for the respective Alpha Levels. We excluded Alpha Levels 1 and 2, because these only apply to the character and word level and are thus not applicable to queries for texts. We henceforth refer to these reading levels as *Alpha readability levels* (Alpha 3 to 6 and above Alpha). We elaborate on our approach in Section 3.3.

3 System Description

KANSAS focuses on the reranking of content queries based on the prioritization of specific grammatical constructions. With this, we follow the approach outlined by Chinkina et al. (2016). For this, we ported some linguistic constructions from *FLAIR* to German and implemented new constructions that are relevant to the contexts of German illiteracy and L2 reading acquisition. Furthermore, we introduced the de-prioritization of grammatical constructions into our system to accommodate for the special needs of adult literacy teaching contexts. As previous systems, we

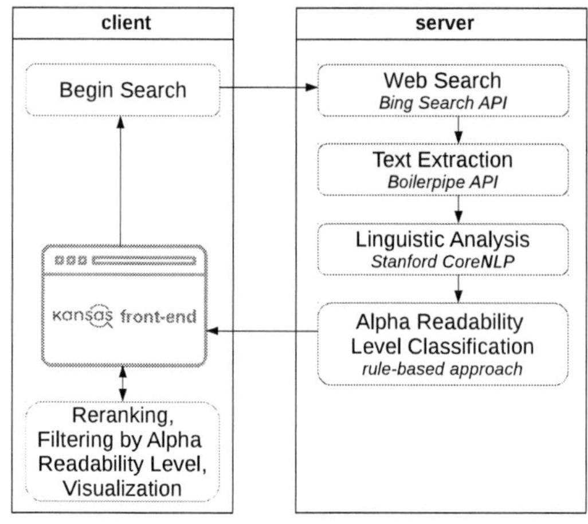

Figure 1: Overview of the KANSAS's workflow.

also provide reading level based filtering of texts. However, unlike previous information retrieval systems, we go beyond simple readability formulas and employ a more linguistically-informed approach to readability assessment.

3.1 Technical Implementation

KANSAS is a web-based application developed in Java using the Google Web Toolkit (GWT). The technical architecture including web search, crawling, parsing, and ranking is based on *FLAIR* (Chinkina et al., 2016): Remote Procedure Calls (RPC) are used for client server communication. The BING Web Search API version 5.0^3 is employed for the web search and the Boilerpipe Java API[4] for text extraction. The linguistic preprocessing is performed using Stanford CoreNLP.[5] The BM25 IR algorithm (Robertson and Walker, 1994) is used to combine the weights for content fit and linguistic constructions. For the front-end design, we use GWT Material Design.[6]

3.2 Workflow

Figure 1 illustrates our system architecture and workflow. While the system's basic architecture strongly resembles the *FLAIR* pipeline described in Chinkina et al. (2016), we did not merely reimplement *FLAIR*. We systematically redesigned the components web search, text extraction, linguistic analysis, and ranking to German, and ex-

---

[2]http://blogs.epb.uni-hamburg.de/lea/,
http://blogs.epb.uni-hamburg.de/leo/.

[3]https://azure.microsoft.com/en-us/services/
cognitive-services/bing-web-search-api/
[4]https://boilerpipe-web.appspot.com/
[5]https://stanfordnlp.github.io/CoreNLP/
[6]https://github.com/GwtMaterialDesign

Level	Reading skills
Alpha 1	pre-literal reading (character level)
Alpha 2	constructs meaning at word level
Alpha 3	constructs meaning at sentence level
Alpha 4	constructs meaning at test level and knows high-frequent words
Alpha 5/6	increasingly literate at intermediate text length

Table 1: Definition of Alpha Levels (cf. Riekmann and Grotlüschen, 2011, p. 28, Table 1).

tended them to the special needs context of adult literacy teaching. Furthermore, we developed a readability filter performing a refined and empirically grounded classification of texts into Alpha readability levels.

Web search. The workflow starts with the client sending a search query to the server. On server side, the BING Web Search API is prompted to query for relevant search results. While *FLAIR* filters these results by discarding all texts containing less than 100 words, we set the lower word limit to 10 words and additionally discard all texts with more than 400 words as these are necessarily unsuited for adult literacy classes.

Text extraction. To remove boilerplate and template strings that do not belong to the websites' main textual content, we make use of the *ArticleExtractor* included in the Boilerpipe Java API. We chose this extractor, which has been trained on news articles, after piloting the performance of all available filters.

Linguistic analysis/preprocessing. We use the Stanford CoreNLP API to extract linguistic annotations from the resulting plain texts. We use the German shift-reduce model for parsing.

Alpha level classification. Based on the linguistic analysis, we compute a set of features to determine a text's Alpha readability level. We assign these levels to texts following a rule-based approach, which is outlined in more detail in Section 3.3 and evaluated in Section 4.2.

Ranking, filtering, and visualization. On the client side, the user is asked to wait until the analysis is completed. Afterwards, the user can inspect the linguistically analyzed query results. Figure 2 shows how the results are displayed to the user: The settings panel on the left contains range sliders that allow the user to set priority weights to a broad range of linguistic constructions. Setting a construction's weight to a negative value penalizes texts containing the construction, while positive values cause higher ranks. Each time a slider

is changed, the results are reranked accordingly and the construction gets highlighted in the text preview window on the right. This may either be used for verification of the automatic analysis or as visual enhancement for teaching purposes. The performance of this feature is evaluated in Section 4.1. Additionally, user may filter query results for certain Alpha readability levels. We also re-implemented *FLAIR*'s visualization perspective which allows to inspect the occurrences of constructions across texts.

3.3 Main Algorithms

KANSAS is based on two main algorithms: The first algorithm concerns the extraction of linguistic constructions from a textual document. This algorithm is relevant for two important functionalities: First, users are given the possibility to rank search results by prioritizing and de-prioritizing certain linguistic constructions. Second, the constructions are visually enhanced within the text preview (cf. Figure 2). The second algorithm classifies texts into Alpha readability levels.

The algorithm for the detection of the constructions is based on our NLP preprocessing pipeline. In total, 85 construction types are annotated on sentence-, phrase-, or token-level based on part-of-speech (POS) annotations and constituency trees. On the sentence-level, we extract sentence types (e.g., simple or complex sentences) and question types (e.g., wh-questions). On the phrase-level, subordinate clause types (e.g., relative clauses) are extracted. On the word-level, we annotate properties of verbs, adjectives, nouns, negations, determiners, pronouns and prepositions. We use Tregex to identify patterns in parse trees based on regular expressions (Levy and Andrew, 2006). While *FLAIR*, too, makes use of Tregex patterns, we newly implemented all patterns to fit the German syntax and POS tags. We excluded constructions that are not relevant for German, such as long and short form adjective comparative con-

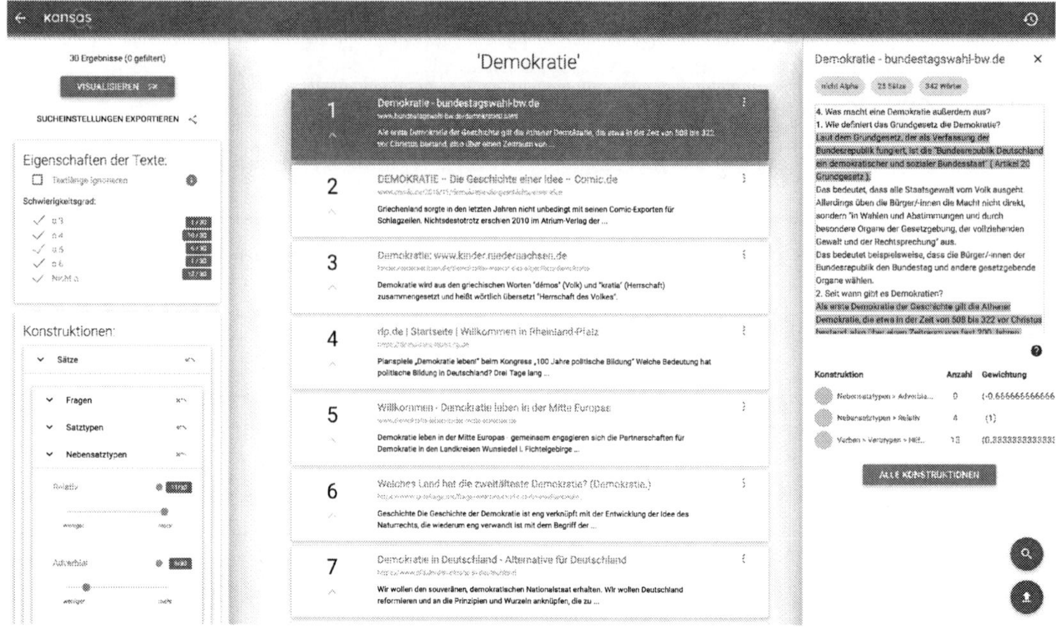

Figure 2: KANSAS's interface: This view displays the search results for the query *Demokratie* ("democracy"). On the settings panel on the left, the user can assign weights to linguistic constructions and filter for Alpha readability levels. The preview panel on the right highlights selected constructions.

structions. We also implemented new constructions that are specifically relevant for the contexts of German and adult literacy classes, such as various constructions used for the elaboration of the German nominal domain and verb position features. The performance of this algorithm is evaluated in sections 4.1.

The second crucial algorithm employed in KANSAS is a sophisticated readability filter for Alpha readability levels. In order to find texts that match the reading skills of the intended target group, we developed a theoretically grounded algorithm to identify readability levels for functional illiterates. We based this rule-based algorithm on the operationalization of criteria for the identification of functional illiteracy levels (Alpha 3 to Alpha 6) (cf. Section 2.3). We used the detailed ability-based descriptions provided by Gausche et al. (2014) and Kretschmann and Wieken (2010) to derive robust operationalizations of each Alpha Level in terms of concrete text characteristics along the dimensions of text length, sentence length, sentence structure, tense patterns, and word length and extract all linguistic features relevant for this assessment from our NLP preprocessing pipeline.[7] We preferred this approach over

one adopting guidelines for Easy-to-Read materials as done in previous work (cf. Section 2.2). Following the ability-based descriptions of degrees of functional illiteracy allows us to differentiate reading levels within the reach of readers with low literacy skills. Furthermore, unlike text production guidelines, German *Alpha Levels* specify concrete thresholds for most of their linguistic characteristics, which allows us to evaluate materials without using reference corpora containing reading materials that were verified to be suited for readers with low literacy skills. This is crucial for our approach given that such corpora are not freely available for German.

4 System Evaluation

We have evaluated both of KANSAS's core algorithms in two pilot studies. First, we tested the performance of our linguistic construction identification algorithm for a subset of five linguistic constructions. Second, we evaluated the performance of our readability assessment algorithm by comparing it to the performance of a human expert annotator.

---

[7]The complete algorithm may be found in the Appendix in Figure 3.

4.1 Identification of Linguistic Constructions

We analyzed five target constructions from our list of overall 85 linguistic constructions. We chose four constructions that are extracted using Tregex patterns, because these are more elaborate and thus more prone to errors. We also chose one construction that is solely based on Stanford CoreNLP POS tags to compare its performance to the other constructions. Furthermore, we only chose constructions that are particularly relevant for adult literacy classes. This resulted in the following target constructions:

Complex sentences are sentences that contain more than one clause, e.g., *Ich spiele und du liest* ("I am playing and you are reading").

***Haben* perfect** is the simple perfect formed with *haben* ("to have"), e.g., *Ich habe geschlafen* ("I have slept").

Participle verbs are verbs in the non-finite form that is used to form periphrastic tenses such as simple perfect and past perfect.

Adjectival attributes are adjectives that are attributes to noun phrases, e.g., *der **grüne** Ball* ("the green ball").

LSB + RSB clauses are clauses that contain at least two verb components which are separated by an arbitrary amount of language material in the center of the clause, e.g., *Sie **hat** in der Mensa **gegessen**.* ("She ate in the canteen").[8]

To evaluate how robustly the algorithm identifies these constructions, we analyzed five to ten articles for each target construction. We performed queries with our system for several search terms and selected the highest ranking of 40 documents after re-ranking the query results by prioritizing the respective target construction.[9] We collected articles until we observed a sufficient amount of instances for each target construction (15 to 59). Table 2 reports precision, recall, and f-measure

for each target construction as well as the amount of observed constructions on which the results are based. On average we observe a satisfactory per-

Construction	N	Prec	Rec	F_1
Complex sentences	43	.788	.953	.863
haben-perfect	15	1.00	.867	.929
Participle verbs	42	.929	.929	.929
Adjectival attributes	59	.946	.593	.729
LSB + RSB	31	.893	.806	.847
Mean score	38	.911	.830	.859

Table 2: Performance of identification of linguistic constructions.

formance across all target constructs. However, the low recall we observe for adjectival noun attributes ($rec. = .593$) indicates that our algorithm may yet be improved. A qualitative analysis of the false negative instances showed that in coordinated adjectival noun attributes the second adjectival attribute is often but not always missed by the algorithm. We are currently investigating the cause for this. However, this issue is less pressing for the system's overall performance, since high precision is more important for the prioritization and visual enhancement of target constructions.

Overall, these preliminary findings are encouraging and give us crucial insights into which aspects of our algorithm require more performance tuning. We are continuing to evaluate all constructions identified by KANSAS and to further improve on our construction identification algorithm.

4.2 Identification of Readability Levels

We conducted a preliminary evaluation of our readability level filter by matching its ratings against human expert judgments in terms of inter-rater reliability. For this, we crawled $N = 68$ texts from websites that offer reading materials for functional illiterates and German L2 learners. We let a human annotate these texts, who was considered an expert because she had extensively studied the ability-based descriptions of functional illiteracy levels by Gausche et al. (2014) and Kretschmann and Wieken (2010) as well as the example material provided by them in the months prior to the annotation procedure. The human annotations were based on annotation guidelines that we derived from the same ability-based Alpha Level descriptions we used for the design of our rule-based algorithm (Weiss and Geppert, 2018).

---

[8]We refer to this type of clause as LSB + RSB clause as a shorthand for left sentence bracket + right sentence bracket clauses, which are names for the respective positions of the verb components in the *Topological Field Model* (Wöllstein, 2014).

[9]We used the following query terms: *Demokratie* ("democracy"), *Bundestag* (the German federal parliament), *Chancengleichheit* ("equal opportunity"), and *Bildungsmassnahme* ("educational measures").

We then automatically rated the same texts with our Alpha readability classifier and calculated the inter-rater reliability (IRR) of the ratings. This procedure allowed us to obtain a preliminary evaluation of the performance of our algorithm despite the lack of a suited Gold Standard.

Before we calculated the IRR, we tested for prevalence using the Stuart Maxwell test for marginal homogeneity but did not find any significant prevalence. We also tested for rater bias by calculating the coefficient of systematic bias between two raters but did not find any significant bias. Accordingly, we calculated Cohen's κ (Cohen, 1960) and observed substantial agreement between the human expert and our algorithm ($\kappa = .63$). We additionally calculated weighted κ_w (Cohen, 1968) in order to account for the ordinal structure in our data. Following Hallgren (2012) we chose quadratic weights to differentiate between degrees of disagreement between two raters. We observe near perfect agreement for quadratic weighted κ ($\kappa_w = .90$). All analyses were conducted using used the R package IRR (v. 0.84).[10]

While the described procedure is only an initial pilot study, which is limited in terms of its validity due to the lack of a second annotator, it already shows highly promising results. We are now addressing the limitations of the pilot by evaluating the robustness of the readability algorithm as well as of our human rater guidelines in a more elaborate study with 300 additional texts rated by two human annotators.

5 Conclusion & Outlook

KANSAS is the first web search engine designed to identify texts for German functional illiterates or German as a Second Language. The system supports the flexible (de)prioritization and visual enhancement of 85 linguistic constructions that are important for German adult literacy teaching and GSL learning contexts. Our theoretically grounded readability algorithm is specifically calibrated towards the needs of functional illiterates. It thus addresses the issue that most reading materials that may be found on the Internet are ill-suited for the special reading needs of functional illiterates.

We presented KANSAS's main features and evaluated its key algorithms in two pilot studies.

Our exemplary analysis of the performance of the identification of linguistic constructions shows a promising overall performance with high f-scores across four out of five constructions ranging from 0.85 to 0.93. The rule-based algorithm which rates the readability of texts was compared with the performance of a human expert annotator. We observed high agreement results with a Cohen's κ value of 0.63 and weighted κ_w of 0.9. We tuned our readability algorithm specifically towards the target group of German functionally illiterates by basing it on the German official criteria for the identification of functional illiteracy levels.

Our pilot studies successfully demonstrate the robustness of our algorithms in real-life applications. The web system is platform-independent and freely available online. While some of the functionality is also featured in previous work on the *FLAIR* system for English, we also provide novel features such as a sophisticated readability filter and the de-prioritization of constructions. Furthermore, this is the first search engine for German functional illiteracy contexts. Due to our incorporation of important insights from SLA research, KANSAS is also suited for the use in GSL contexts.

Our next steps include to further refine KANSAS's performance and to conduct more elaborate evaluation studies for both algorithms. Furthermore, we are currently conducting usability studies in which teaching practitioners from the fields of adult literacy and GSL acquisition are evaluating KANSAS in terms of its suitability for real-life use.

Acknowledgments

We are grateful to our project partners Theresa Geppert, Hannes Schröter, and Josef Schrader of the German Institute for Adult Education – Leibniz Centre for Lifelong Learning (DIE) for their valuable collaboration. We also thank the anonymous reviewers for their insightful suggestions.

KANSAS is a research and development project funded by the Federal Ministry of Education and Research (BMBF) as part of the *AlphaDekade*[11] [grant number W143500].

---

[10] https://cran.r-project.org/web/packages/irr/

[11] https://www.alphadekade.de/

References

Rebekah George Benjamin. 2012. Reconstructing readability: Recent developments and recommendations in the analysis of text difficulty. *Educational Psychology Review*, 24:63–88.

Jonathan Brown and Maxine Eskenazi. 2004. Retrieval of authentic documents for reader-specific lexical practice. In *InSTIL/ICALL Symposium 2004*.

Tim Vor der Brück, Sven Hartrumpf, and Hermann Helbig. 2008. A readability checker with supervised learning using deep syntactic and semantic indicators. *Informatica*, 32(4):429–435.

Jeanne S. Chall and Edgar Dale. 1995. *Readability revisited: the new Dale-Chall Readability Formula*. Brookline Books.

Xiaobin Chen and Detmar Meurers. 2017. Word frequency and readability: Predicting the text-level readability with a lexical-level attribute. *Journal of Research in Reading*, 41(3):486–510.

Maria Chinkina, Madeeswaran Kannan, and Detmar Meurers. 2016. Online information retrieval for language learning. In *Proceedings of ACL-2016 System Demonstrations*, pages 7–12, Berlin, Germany. Association for Computational Linguistics.

Jacob Cohen. 1960. A coefficient of agreement for nominal scales. *Educational and Psychological Measurement*, 20(1):37–46.

Jacob Cohen. 1968. Weighted kappa: Nominal scale agreement provision for scaled disagreement or partial credit. *Psychological Bulletin*, 70(4):213–220.

Scott A. Crossley, David B. Allen, and Danielle McNamara. 2011. Text readability and intuitive simplification: A comparison of readability formulas. *Reading in a Foreign Language*, 23(1):84–101.

Scott A. Crossley, Jerry Greenfield, and Danielle S. Mcnamara. 2008. Assessing text readability using cognitively based indices. *TESOL Quarterly*, 42(3):475–493.

Felice Dell'Orletta, Simonetta Montemagni, and Giulia Venturi. 2011. Read-it: Assessing readability of Italian texts with a view to text simplification. In *Proceedings of the 2nd Workshop on Speech and Language Processing for Assistive Technologies*, pages 73–83.

William H. DuBay. 2006. *The Classic Readability Studies*. Impact Information, Costa Mesa, California.

Sukru Eraslan, Victoria Yaneva, and Yeliz Yelisada. 2017. Do web users with autism experience barriers when searching for information within web pages? In *Proceedings of the 14th Web for All Conference on The Future of Accessible Work*, pages 20–23. ACM.

B. Janghorban Esfahani, A. Faron, K. S. Roth, P. P. Grimminger, and J. C. Luers. 2016. Systematic readability analysis of medical texts on websites of german university clinics for general and abdominal surgery. *Zentralblatt fur Chirurgie*, 141(6):639–644.

Lijun Feng. 2009. Automatic readability assessment for people with intellectual disabilities. In *ACM SIGACCESS accessibility and computing*, volume 93, pages 84–91.

Lijun Feng, Noémie Elhadad, and Matt Huenerfauth. 2009. Cognitively motivated features for readability assessment. In *Proceedings of the 12th Conference of the European Chapter of the ACL (EACL 2009)*, pages 229–237, Athens, Greece. Association for Computational Linguistics.

Lijun Feng, Martin Jansche, Matt Huenerfauth, and Noémie Elhadad. 2010. A comparison of features for automatic readability assessment. *Proceedings of the 23rd International Conference on Computational Linguistics*, pages 276–284.

Thomas François and Cedrick Fairon. 2012. An "AI readability" formula for French as a foreign language. In *Proceedings of the 2012 Joint Conference on Empirical Methods in Natural Language Processing and Computational Natural Language Learning*.

Geert Freyhoff, Gerhard Hess, Linda Kerr, Elizabeth Menzell, Bror Tronbacke, and Kathy Van Der Veken. 1998. *Make It Simple, European Guidelines for the Production of Easy-to-Read Information for People with Learning Disability for authors, editors, information providers, translators and other interested persons*. International League of Societies for Persons with Mental Handicap European Association, Brussels.

Mark G. Friedman and Diane Nelson Bryen. 2007. Web accessibility design recommendations for people with cognitive disabilities. *Technology and Disability*, 19(4):205–212.

Silke Gausche, Anne Haase, and Diana Zimper. 2014. *Lesen. DVV-Rahmencurriculum*, 1 edition. Deutscher Volkshochschul-Verband e.V., Bonn.

Petronella Grootens-Wiegers, Martine C. De Vries, Tessa E. Vossen, and Jos M. Van den Broek. 2015. Readability and visuals in medical research information forms for children and adolescents. *Science Communication*, 37(1):89–117.

Kevin A. Hallgren. 2012. Computing inter-rater reliability for observational data: An overview and tutorial. *Tutorials in quantitative methods for psychology*, 8(1):23–34.

Julia Hancke, Detmar Meurers, and Sowmya Vajjala. 2012. Readability classification for German using lexical, syntactic, and morphological features. In *Proceedings of the 24th International Conference on*

Computational Linguistics (COLING), pages 1063–1080, Mumbay, India.

Matt Huenerfauth, Lijun Feng, and Noémie Elhadad. 2009. Comparing evaluation techniques for text readability software for adults with intellectual disabilities. In *Proceedings of the 11th international ACM SIGACCESS conference on Computers and accessibility*, Assets '09, pages 3–10, New York, NY, USA. ACM.

J. Peter Kincaid, Robert P. Fishburne, Richard L. Rogers, and Brad S. Chissom. 1975. Derivation of new readability formulas (Automated Readability Index, Fog Count and Flesch Reading Ease formula) for Navy enlisted personnel. Research Branch Report 8-75, Naval Technical Training Command, Millington, TN.

Stephen Krashen. 1977. Some issues relating to the monitor model. *On Tesol*, 77(144-158).

Rudolf Kretschmann and Petra Wieken. 2010. *Lesen. Alpha Levels*. lea., Hamburg.

Roger Levy and Galen Andrew. 2006. Tregex and tsurgeon: tools for querying and manipulating tree data structures. In *Proceedings of the fifth international conference on Language Resources and Evaluation*, pages 2231–2234, Genoa, Italy. European Language Resources Association (ELRA).

Luís Marujo, José Lopes, Nuno Mamede, Isabel Trancoso, Juan Pino, Maxine Eskenazi, Jorge Baptista, and Céu Viana. 2009. Porting reap to european portuguese. In *International Workshop on Speech and Language Technology in Education*.

Jacob E. McCarthy and Sarah J. Swierenga. 2010. What we know about dyslexia and web accessibility: a research review. *Universal Access in the Information Society*, 9(2):147–152.

Detmar Meurers, Ramon Ziai, Luiz Amaral, Adriane Boyd, Aleksandar Dimitrov, Vanessa Metcalf, and Niels Ott. 2010. Enhancing authentic web pages for language learners. In *Proceedings of the 5th Workshop on Innovative Use of NLP for Building Educational Applications (BEA)*, pages 10–18, Los Angeles. ACL.

Eleni Miltsakaki and Audrey Troutt. 2007. Read-x: Automatic evaluation of reading difficulty of web text. In *E-Learn: World Conference on E-Learning in Corporate, Government, Healthcare, and Higher Education*, pages 7280–7286. Association for the Advancement of Computing in Education (AACE).

Misako Nomura, Gyda Skat Nielsen, and Bror Tronbacke. 2010. Guidelines for easy-to-read materials. revision on behalf of the ifla/library services to people with special needs section. IFLA Professional Reports 120, International Federation of Library Associations and Institutions, The Hague, IFLA Headquarters.

Niels Ott and Detmar Meurers. 2011. Information retrieval for education: Making search engines language aware. *Themes in Science and Technology Education*, 3(1-2):9–30.

Luz Rello, Ricardo Baeza-Yates, Laura Dempere-Marco, and Horacio Saggion. 2013a. Frequent words improve readability and short words improve understandability for people with dyslexia. In *IFIP Conference on Human-Computer Interaction*, pages 203–219, Berlin, Heidelberg. Springer.

Luz Rello, Susana Bautista, Ricardo Baeza-Yates, Pablo Gervás, Raquel Hervás, and Horacio Saggion. 2013b. One half or 50%? an eye-tracking study of number representation readability. In *IFIP Conference on Human-Computer Interaction*, pages 229–245, Berlin, Heidelberg. Springer.

Wibke Riekmann and Anke Grotlüschen. 2011. Konservative Entscheidungen: Größenordnung des funktionalen Analphabetismus in Deutschland. *REPORT - Zeitschrift für Weiterbildungsforschung*, 3:24–35.

Stephen E Robertson and Steve Walker. 1994. Some simple effective approximations to the 2-poisson model for probabilistic weighted retrieval. In *Proceedings of the 17th annual international ACM SIGIR conference on Research and development in information retrieval*, pages 232–241. Springer-Verlag New York, Inc.

Richard W. Schmidt. 1990. The role of consciousness in second language learning. *Applied Linguistics*, 11:206–226.

Michael Sharwood Smith. 1993. Input enhancement in instructed SLA. *Studies in Second Language Acquisition*, 15(2):165–179.

Merrill Swain. 1985. Communicative competence: Some roles of comprehensible input and comprehensible output in its development. In Susan M. Gass and Carolyn G. Madden, editors, *Input in second language acquisition*, pages 235–253. Newbury House, Rowley, MA.

Sowmya Vajjala and Detmar Meurers. 2012. On improving the accuracy of readability classification using insights from second language acquisition. In *Proceedings of the 7th Workshop on Innovative Use of NLP for Building Educational Applications (BEA)*, pages 163–173, Montréal, Canada. ACL.

Sowmya Vajjala and Detmar Meurers. 2013. On the applicability of readability models to web texts. In *Proceedings of the Second Workshop on Predicting and Improving Text Readability for Target Reader Populations*, pages 59–68.

Zarah Weiss and Theresa Geppert. 2018. *Textlesbarkeit für Alpha-Levels. Annotationsrichtlinien für Lesetexte*. http://sfs.uni-tuebingen.de/~zweiss/rsrc/textlesbarkeit-fur-alpha.pdf, Bonn, Tübingen.

Zarah Weiss and Detmar Meurers. 2018. Modeling the readability of German targeting adults and children: An empirically broad analysis and its cross-corpus validation. In *Proceedings of the 27th International Conference on Computational Linguistics (Coling 2018)*, Santa Fe, New Mexico, USA. International Committee on Computational Linguistic.

Angelika Wöllstein. 2014. *Topologisches Satzmodell*, 2 edition. Winter, Heidelberg.

Victoria Yaneva. 2015. Easy-read documents as a gold standard for evaluation of text simplification output. In *Proceedings of the Student Research Workshop*, pages 30–36.

Victoria Yaneva, Irina Temnikova, and Ruslan Mitkov. 2015. Accessible texts for autism: An eye-tracking study. In *Proceedings of the 17th International ACM SIGACCESS Conference on Computers & Accessibility*, pages 49–57. ACM.

Victoria Yaneva, Irina Temnikova, and Ruslan Mitkov. 2016. Evaluating the readability of text simplification output for readers with cognitive disabilities. In *Proceedings of the 10h International Conference on Language Resources and Evaluation*, pages 293–299.

A   Appendices

$\downarrow$A\H$\rightarrow$	$\alpha3$	$\alpha4$	$\alpha5$	$\alpha6$	above α
$\alpha3$	22	7	0	0	0
$\alpha4$	3	4	0	2	0
$\alpha5$	0	0	10	0	0
$\alpha6$	0	0	1	6	3
above α	0	0	2	0	8

Table 3: Raw annotation counts for readability assessment performance pilot (A: algorithm; H: human).

```java
/**
 * Assign Alpha readability level given computed features
 *
 * @return DocumentReadabilityLevel The document's Alpha readability level
 */
public DocumentReadabilityLevel computeReadabilityLevel() {
        if (wordsPerSentence <= 10
                && nSentences <= 5
                && syllablesPerToken <= 3
                && pastPerfectsPerFiniteVerb == 0
                && future1sPerFiniteVerb == 0
                && future2sPerFiniteVerb == 0
                && depClausesPerSentence <= 0.5
                && presentPerfectsPerFiniteVerb <= 0.5
                && typesFoundInSubtlexPerLexicalType >= 0.95) {

                alphaLevel = LEVEL_3;

        } else if (wordsPerSentence <= 10
                && nSentences <= 10
                && syllablesPerToken <= 5
                && pastPerfectsPerFiniteVerb == 0
                && future1sPerFiniteVerb == 0
                && future2sPerFiniteVerb == 0) {

                alphaLevel = LEVEL_4;

        } else if (wordsPerSentence <= 12
                && nSentences <= 15
                && pastPerfectsPerFiniteVerb == 0) {

                alphaLevel = LEVEL_5;

        } else if (wordsPerSentence <= 12
                && nSentences <= 20) {

                alphaLevel = LEVEL_6;

        } else {

                alphaLevel = LEVEL_N;

        }

        return alphaLevel;
}
```

Figure 3: A Java code snippet of the algorithm that assigns Alpha readability levels to texts given features such as the number of words per sentence or the number of syllables per token.

Feedback Strategies for Form and Meaning
in a Real-life Language Tutoring System

Ramon Ziai   Björn Rudzewitz
Kordula De Kuthy   Florian Nuxoll   Detmar Meurers

Collaborative Research Center 833
Department of Linguistics, ICALL Research Group[*]
LEAD Graduate School & Research Network
University of Tübingen

Abstract

We describe ongoing work on an English language tutoring system currently being used as part of regular instruction in twelve German high school classes. In contrast to the traditional ICALL system approach analyzing learner language, we build on the approach of Rudzewitz et al. (2018) to generate variants of target answers based on task and target language models and combine this offline step with an online process flexibly matching learner answers with these variants. We extend the approach by advancing the search engine used in the online step to return more relevant results. Then we extend the approach to meaning-focused feedback, showing how it can be realized in the system in addition to the form-focused feedback. We conclude with an outlook on an intervention study we have designed to evaluate the system.

1   Introduction

Second Language Acquisition (SLA) has long recognized the need for immediate feedback on learner production (Mackey, 2006). However, in real-life classrooms, there is limited opportunity for such immediate feedback if every student is to be considered according to her needs.

Intelligent Language Tutoring Systems make it possible to address this shortcoming since they offer the possibility of automated, immediate feedback while the learner is working on the task, and many students can use the system at the same time whenever they want to, whereas opportunities for interaction with a teacher or other tutor are much more limited.

However, in order to provide accurate, helpful feedback, the erroneous forms produced by learners need to be characterized. If one analyzes learner language directly, one runs into the problem that state-of-the-art NLP is not equipped to deal with non-standard language in a way that supports fine-grained feedback. This is not surprising given that the linguistic categories system was developed for well-formed, native language, thus NLP tools generally treat the analysis of learner language as a robustness problem, covering up the type of deviation or error that the learner produced instead of characterizing it (Díaz Negrillo et al., 2010; Meurers and Dickinson, 2017). As an example, consider that a standard POS tagger would typically assign the tag VBD to the overregularized form *teached* based on the suffix analysis fallback strategy commonly used for unknown words.

If we know what task the learner language was produced for, this challenge can be addressed to some degree: instead of analyzing the learner productions directly, one can start out from the expected target forms and systematically transform them into well-formed and ill-formed variations of the target (Rudzewitz et al., 2018).

In this paper, we expand on that idea and present feedback strategies supporting both form- and meaning-oriented tasks. After reviewing the process responsible for generating the well-formed and ill-formed variation, we zoom in on the search process executed at feedback time, outlining how standard search engine technology was adapted to serve the needs of a language tutoring system. We show how the same basis of generated variation can support meaning-oriented feedback, using an alignment-based approach inspired by research on Short Answer Assessment (Meurers et al., 2011). We demonstrate this with feedback for reading and listening comprehension where the learner is pointed to the relevant source of information in

---

[*] http://icall-research.de

Ramon Ziai, Bjoern Rudzewitz, Kordula De Kuthy, Florian Nuxoll and Detmar Meurers 2018. Feedback strategies for form and meaning in a real-life language tutoring system. *Proceedings of the 7th Workshop on NLP for Computer Assisted Language Learning at SLTC 2018 (NLP4CALL 2018)*. Linköping Electronic Conference Proceedings 152: 91–98.

the task material. We conclude with an outlook on the design of an intervention study we are currently running in twelve 7th grade classrooms in Germany.

2 System Setup

The feedback strategies discussed in this article are implemented as part of a web-based online workbook, the FeedBook (Rudzewitz et al., 2018; Meurers et al., 2018). The foreign language tutoring system is an adaptation of a paper workbook for a 7th grade English textbook approved for use in German high schools.

Figure 1 provides an authentic example of a student solution to an exercise in the printed workbook on the use of type II conditionals. For such paper-based exercises, feedback is typically given in a delayed fashion by the teacher, when discussing the exercise summarily in class or sometimes by returning marked-up exercise sheets, not while the student is actually thinking about and working on the task.

In contrast, the system we describe provides an interface for students to select and interactively work on exercises. For exercises that aim at teaching grammar topics, students receive automatic, immediate feedback by the system informing them whether their answer is correct (via a green check mark) or *why* their answer is incorrect (via red color, highlighting of the error span, and a metalinguistic feedback message). In fact, rather than pointing out the error as such, we instead formulate scaffolding feedback messages designed to guide the learner towards the solution, without giving it away.

The process of entering an answer and receiving feedback can be repeated, incrementally leading the student to the correct answer. If there are multiple errors in a learner response, the system presents the feedback one at a time. Figure 2 shows the same learner production we saw in Figure 1 together with the interactive feedback immediately provided by the system after this is typed in.

Students can save and resume work, interact with the system to receive automatic feedback and revise their answers, and eventually submit their final solutions to the teacher. In case the answers in a given exercise are all correct, the system grades the submission automatically, without requiring teacher interaction.

For those answers that are not correct with respect to a given target answer, the teacher can manually annotate the learner answer with feedback parallel to the traditional mark-up process known from printed workbooks. Any such manual feedback is saved in a feedback memory and suggested automatically to the teacher in case the form occurs in another learner response to this exercise.

The system also provides students with automatic, immediate feedback for many exercise types, where they traditionally would either not receive it or only after long delay resulting from collecting and manually marking up homework assignments. From the teacher's perspective, the system relieves them from very repetitive and time-consuming work. The exercises are embedded in a full web application with a messaging system for communication, a profile management including e-mail settings, tutorials for using the system, classroom management, and various functions orthogonal to the NLP-related issues.

3 Hypothesis Generation Revisited

The generation of well-formed and ill-formed answers expected for a given exercise builds on the generation framework proposed by Rudzewitz et al. (2018) which generate variants of target answers for each task that one wants to provide feedback for.

The crucial components of the framework are i) a set of rules organized in layers that transform one variant to another variant, introducing one change at a time, ii) a common representation format for adding, removing and querying units of linguistic analysis (the CAS, see Götz and Suhre 2004), and iii) a breadth-first search algorithm that traverses the rule layers, applying rules and passing the output variants of rules to rules in the next layer along with their linguistic analysis.

The setup consists of four layers: in the first layer normalizations like contractions are performed. In the second layer transformations are conducted that yield linguistically well-formed, but task-inappropriate forms like tense changes. As the next step, the third layer introduces changes that result in morphologically ill-formed answers, for example regular endings for irregular verbs in the simple past. Finally, the fourth layer rejoins and normalizes different generated variants. Not every layer introduces new diagnoses: for

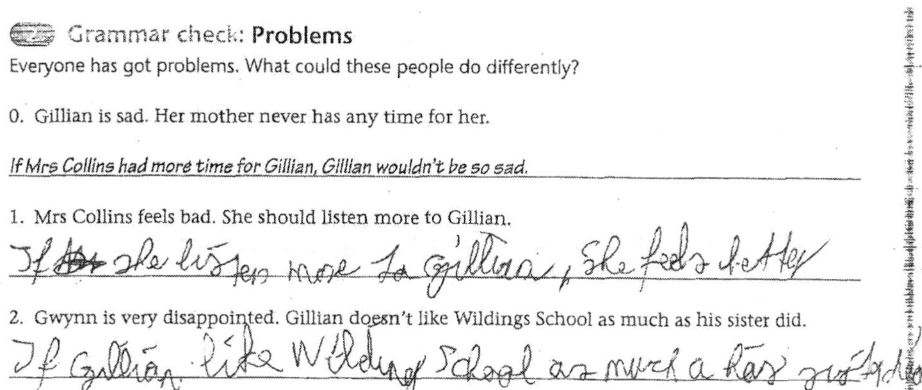

Figure 1: Traditional paper-based exercise

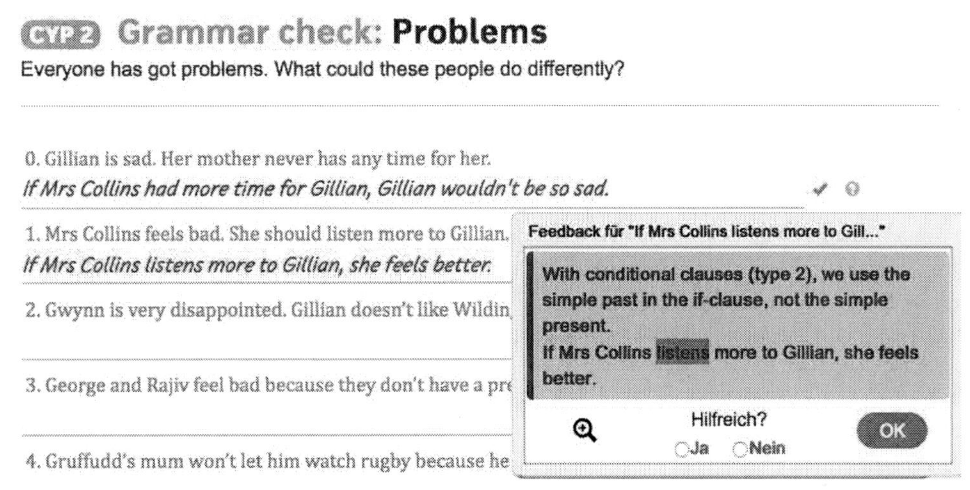

Figure 2: Interactive exercise with form-oriented feedback

the normalization rules, the previous diagnoses are passed on. At each point, the current variant and corresponding analysis is saved so they can be used later for feedback. The system (at the time of publication) generated 95.386 distinct hypotheses for 3.211 target answers.

Table 1 provides some example derivations that result from rule interactions.

4 The Search Mechanism

Given the generation approach outlined in the previous section, it should come as no surprise that especially for short-answer tasks such as the one in Figure 2, the number of generated variants can get very large. This is especially true for items with multiple target answers given that a separate calculation is done for every target answer.

When a learner uses the system and triggers the feedback mechanism for a given item, it is necessary to compare the learner answer to the relevant pre-stored generated variants, determine whether the student made one of the errors present (and thus known to the system) in the variant, and if so, provide feedback. Since it is infeasible to traverse and compare all variants, Rudzewitz et al. (2018) use the search engine framework Lucene[1] to efficiently index and query the stored variants. Every variant is treated like a document indexed by Lucene.

In examining the feedback behavior of such a system, we noticed that Lucene did not always return the most relevant variant for a given learner answer and task. Looking further into this issue, we discovered that this behavior was due to the term weighting scheme used by Lucene and other search engines, known as TF-IDF (Salton and McGill, 1983). TF-IDF works by balancing the frequency of a word in a given document (TF) against the inverse frequency of the word occurring over the whole set of documents (IDF), resulting in low values for very frequent words, and high values for topic-specific words only occurring in few documents.

While this is the desired behavior when looking for specific content, it is not suitable for the present problem of finding relevant variants for learner answers. We therefore modified the approach of Rudzewitz et al. (2018) by i) eliminating the IDF part of the weighting scheme, and ii)

introducing task-specific term weighting into the search.

In order to realize the latter, we draw on information gathered during the generation process. We always store the transformation result r of a rule application, i.e., the part of a variant which was changed by the rule. So the set of all transformation results R is known before the learner interacts with the system. We can thus look for instances of each $r \in R$ of a given task and item (such as the incorrect tense forms shown in Table 1) in the learner answer and assign a higher weight for parts of the learner answer that match r. The weighting is implemented using a Lucene feature called "query boosting", which allows for assignment of different weights to sub-strings of the query. We use the same weight for all matches (currently 5.0), whereas the non-matched answer parts receive the standard weight of 1.0.

As a result of this modification, the system is able to give more task-relevant feedback for the learner answer in Figure 2 despite a low token overlap of the learner answer with the target answer. In order to also obtain a quantitative result, we ran the new search mechanism against the same data used for coverage testing in Rudzewitz et al. (2018): we observed a 6% increase in types of answers covered by construction-specific feedback (16.9% / 1085 instances vs. 10.9% / 696 instances) as a consequence of the search mechanism introduced above.

5 Meaning-oriented Feedback

Depending on the nature of the exercise, it is essential to draw the learners' attention not just to forms but also to content-related misconceptions. Indeed, for meaning-based exercises such as listening- or reading comprehension, feedback on meaning should take priority over feedback on form. The strategies needed to detect such errors are very different from the ones used for the form-oriented feedback described so far. In contrast to analyzing or generating variation in form, one needs to abstract over it and recognize meaning equivalence of different forms. A learner answer can then be accepted as correct whenever meaning equivalence has been established between it and the target answer.

There is a vast body of work on automated short-answer grading (see Burrows et al. 2015 for an overview), but the overwhelming majority of

---

[1] https://lucene.apache.org/core/

target	layer 1	layer 2	layer 3
are you doing	are you doing	are you doing	are you doing
	were you doing	were you do	was you do
	have you been doing	have you been do	have you been dos
	had you been doing	had you been do	had you been dos
	will you do	are you do	will you dos
	did you do	…	did you dos
	…		are you dos
			was you doing
			is you dos
			is you doing
			…
friendlier	friendlier	friendlier	friendlier
	more friendly	more friendlier	most friendlier
	friendlyer	more friendlyer	most friendlyer
	…		friendliest
		…	friendlyest
			…

Table 1: Examples for generated answer variants

work only lends itself to the task of holistically scoring learner answers, not detecting the type of divergence from target answers. We chose to adapt the alignment-based CoMiC system (Meurers et al., 2011) to our needs. Instead of classifying learner productions, we use the alignment information from CoMiC as evidence for equivalence or divergence (e.g., missing information) of the learner answer from the target answer.

Given the means of detecting meaning errors, the question arises how to point the student in the right direction. Since it is pedagogically not acceptable to reveal (parts of) the correct answer, an alternate means of scaffolding for meaning-oriented exercises such as reading and listening comprehension is needed. How can this be done?

Our general approach is to draw the learner's attention to relevant parts of the task context. This can be a part of the reading text or listening clip, the question being asked, or the instruction text. Figure 3 shows feedback on a learner answer with missing information. The system reacts to the problem by visually highlighting the relevant part of the reading text, pointing the learner into the direction of the correct answer.

For listening comprehension exercises, the overall strategy is the same, but instead of highlighting or displaying text, we provide an excerpt of the corresponding audio clip that contains the information necessary for answering the given question. Figure 4 illustrates an example for such feedback. Since the current number of suitable tasks in FeedBook is limited, a teacher from the project team manually specified the relevant part of the task context for each task. In the future, we plan to automatically identify these information sources in reading texts or transcripts of listening texts. Furthermore, we are in the process of compiling a test suite for meaning-oriented feedback in order to quantitatively evaluate our approach.

6 Summary

We presented extensions to the language tutoring system FeedBook currently in use in English 7th grade classrooms. The extensions are i) a task-based optimization of the search strategy necessary when comparing learner answers to pre-stored variants and ii) the addition of meaning-oriented scaffolding feedback for reading and listening activities. We demonstrated both extensions by example. The first extension shows that if the task is known and target answers exist, it is possible to give accurate feedback on learner language without having to directly process it. The second extension makes it possible to give helpful, pedagogically sound scaffolding feedback on meaning-oriented tasks.

7 Outlook: Towards a Large-Scale Intervention Study

Moving forward, it will be necessary to evaluate the effectiveness of the system in terms of learning outcomes. Very few ICALL systems have been evaluated in real-life formal learning contexts (for some notable exceptions, cf. Nagata, 1996; Heift, 2004, 2010; Choi, 2016), let alone in terms of standards for intervention studies established in psychology and empirical educational science. However, in order to raise awareness for and show the impact of ICALL systems, it arguably is crucial

James is a student at St David's College. Read his report and answer the questions below.

1. How did James feel when he first came to St David's?
I don't know

Figure 3: Meaning-oriented feedback for reading comprehension exercise

B7 Talking to Gwynn

b) Listen again and complete the statements in 1 to 3 words.

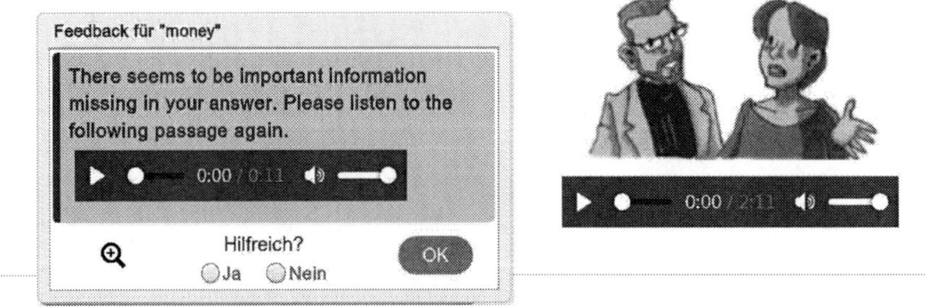

Gwynn tells Mrs Collins that Gillian needs *money* ✖ ❶ ❷ to get used to the situation.

Figure 4: Meaning-oriented feedback for listening comprehension exercise

to provide large-scale evaluation in terms of externally established measures of learning outcomes. In our case, we want to measure the impact of interactive feedback on the individual learning outcomes of 7th grade school children.

We have set up a randomized controlled field study that compares two groups of students receiving immediate feedback on different grammatical constructions throughout the current school year. The variables that are relevant to control in such a context include: a) the learners' language proficiency, b) individual differences in aptitude/cognition, c) motivational factors, and, last but far from least, d) the teacher, known to have the strongest influence on learning outcome in classrooms.

For a), we plan to administer both a C-Test measuring general language proficiency as well as a construction-specific grammar test geared towards testing grammar topics that are part of the 7th grade English curriculum. When piloting the grammar test, we observed that conducting a systematic pre-test of all constructions at the beginning of the school year, before the students have covered these constructions in class, is very time consuming and leads to significant student frustration. Students are not used to being tested on material they have not systematically covered in school yet. So for the main study, we are distributing the pre-tests of the grammatical constructions throughout the school year to just before the specific construction is being covered in class.

In order to control for b), we will employ established individual difference tests such as MLAT-5 (Carroll and Sapon, 1959) to determine fixed traits of learners, such as working memory capacity. For motivation and other background traits (c), we will use a questionnaire where students answer a range of questions on the subject they learn, the languages they speak, and other relevant information. Originally, we had planned to administer all these tests using our web-based platform. To ensure that these tests are conducted systematically, this is supposed to happen in class.

It turns out, however, that in the current state of the German secondary school system, the overhead of scheduling classes in computer rooms providing a sufficient number of computers that are functional and connected to the Internet is a significant burden for teachers. Conducting tests on paper, on the other hand, means having to manually enter the data later, which for studies of this size is very work intensive and error prone. For some of the individual difference tests, it is possible, though, to let students complete them at home using the digital device they also use to access the tutoring system. In pilot testing some tests in such a way outside of class, we found that in such a setting it is very difficult to ensure that all students actually complete the tests. To enforce completion, in the main study we are only making the interactive online exercises for the next chapter available in the tutoring system once the tests scheduled at that point have been completed by a student.

To account for the teacher factor (d), the intervention study uses within-class randomization. We divided the grammar topics in the curriculum into two groups and assign students randomly to one of these groups. Students get immediate system feedback on the constructions assigned to their group, while not receiving automated feedback on the other grammar topics. Both groups thus receive feedback from the system, but systematically for different constructions. If the interactive feedback is effective, the two student groups should differ in their performance on the different grammatical construction and general language proficiency posttest. Except for the presumably stable traits, such as working memory and the background and motivation questionnaires, all tests are administered following a pre-/posttest design.

In addition to the twelve test classes with within-class randomization, we also recruited a separate class as a business-as-usual control, where the traditional paper workbook is used and only the tests are administered. We intentionally did not make the comparison with business-as-usual the main focus of our study since we want to determine the effect of interactive scaffolding feedback on learning, not the well-known newness effect of using a web-based computer system in comparison to a paper-based workbook.

Acknowledgements

We are grateful to the high school students, parents and teachers using the FeedBook system and providing much useful feedback. We would also like to thank the reviewers for their detailed and helpful comments.

References

Steven Burrows, Iryna Gurevych, and Benno Stein. 2015. The eras and trends of automatic short answer grading. *International Journal of Artificial Intelligence in Education*, 25(1):60–117.

John B. Carroll and Stanley M. Sapon. 1959. *Modern language aptitude test*. Psychological Corporation, San Antonio, TX, US.

Inn-Chull Choi. 2016. Efficacy of an ICALL tutoring system and process-oriented corrective feedback. *Computer Assisted Language Learning*, 29(2):334–364.

Ana Díaz Negrillo, Detmar Meurers, Salvador Valera, and Holger Wunsch. 2010. Towards interlanguage POS annotation for effective learner corpora in SLA and FLT. *Language Forum*, 36(1–2):139–154.

Thilo Götz and Oliver Suhre. 2004. Design and implementation of the uima common analysis system. *IBM Systems Journal*, 43(3):476–489.

Trude Heift. 2004. Corrective feedback and learner uptake in call. *ReCALL*, 16(2):416–431.

Trude Heift. 2010. Prompting in CALL: A longitudinal study of learner uptake. *Modern Language Journal*, 94(2):198–216.

Alison Mackey. 2006. Feedback, noticing and instructed second language learning. *Applied Linguistics*, 27(3):405–430.

Detmar Meurers and Markus Dickinson. 2017. Evidence and interpretation in language learning research: Opportunities for collaboration with computational linguistics. *Language Learning*, 67(2).

Detmar Meurers, Kordula De Kuthy, Verena Möller, Florian Nuxoll, Björn Rudzewitz, and Ramon Ziai. 2018. Digitale Differenzierung benötigt Informationen zu Sprache, Aufgabe und Lerner. Zur Generierung von individuellem Feedback in einem interaktiven Arbeitsheft [Digitial differentiation requires information on language, task, and learner. On the generation of individual feedback in an interactive workbook]. *FLuL – Fremdsprachen Lehren und Lernen*, 47(2):64–82.

Detmar Meurers, Ramon Ziai, Niels Ott, and Stacey Bailey. 2011. Integrating parallel analysis modules to evaluate the meaning of answers to reading comprehension questions. *IJCEELL. Special Issue on Automatic Free-text Evaluation*, 21(4):355–369.

Noriko Nagata. 1996. Computer vs. workbook instruction in second language acquistion. *CALICO Journal*, 14(1):53–75.

Björn Rudzewitz, Ramon Ziai, Kordula De Kuthy, Verena Möller, Florian Nuxoll, and Detmar Meurers. 2018. Generating feedback for English foreign language exercises. In *Proceedings of the 13th Workshop on Innovative Use of NLP for Building Educational Applications (BEA)*, pages 127–136. ACL.

Gerard Salton and Michael J. McGill. 1983. *Introduction to modern information retrieval*. McGraw-Hill, New York.

Association for Computational Linguistics
209 N. Eighth Street
Stroudsburg, Pennsylvania 18360

ISBN 978-1-5108-7752-8